EATING THE BIBLE

EATING THE BIBLE

Over 50 Delicious Recipes to Feed Your Body and Nourish Your Soul

RENA ROSSNER
PHOTOGRAPHS BY BOAZ LAVI

Skyhorse Publishing

Skyhorse Publishing books may be purchased in bulk at special discounts for sales promotion, corporate gifts, fund-raising, or educational purposes. Special editions can also be created to specifications. For details, contact the Special Sales Department, Skyhorse Publishing, 307 West 36th Street, 11th Floor, New York, NY 10018 or info@skyhorsepublishing.com.

Skyhorse® and Skyhorse Publishing® are registered trademarks of Skyhorse Publishing, Inc.®, a Delaware corporation.

Visit our website at www.skyhorsepublishing.com.

10 9 8 7 6 5 4 3 2 1

Library of Congress Cataloging-in-Publication Data is available on file.

Cover design by Brian Peterson
Cover photo credit Boaz Lavi

ISBN: 978-1-5107-0649-1
Ebook ISBN: 978-1-62873-463-8

Printed in China

Your children should be like olive plants around your table.
Psalms 128:3

To my parents

Contents

Introduction

If the way to a man's heart is through his stomach, perhaps
the palate can light the way to the soul.

One weekend, almost ten years ago, I was served a bowl of lentil soup at a Friday night dinner. The weekly portion of the Bible that had been read that week in synagogue was the chapter in which Esau sells his birthright to his brother Jacob for a bowl of red lentil soup. The ability to bring the Bible alive in such a tactile way motivated me to begin work on a cookbook, entitled *Eating the Bible*. The recipes I've gathered serve as talking points for conversation, and as a fun and meaningful way to incorporate the Bible into a weekly meal.

This cookbook is an innovative addition to the kitchen, not only because it will change table conversation and make every meal into an experience as tactile as any holiday, but because it is a cookbook that enriches the soul of the cook along with the palates of those at her table. Every cook must glance at a recipe countless times before completing a dish. Often recipes involve five- to ten-minute periods during which one must wait for the water to boil, the soup to simmer, or the onions to sauté. It is my goal to help enrich those moments with biblical verse and commentary to enable cooks to feed their souls as they work to feed the members of their households.

But the reason this cookbook is so dynamic is that it does not stop at the cook. The tidbits of knowledge the cook gains while cooking can not only be shared with guests and family, but the food itself becomes an item for discussion. I hope that *Eating the Bible* will change the way we cook and the way we eat.

The Recipes

Eating the Bible began with a bowl of lentil soup, but it also began with a notebook. I spent years jotting down ideas and concepts

that came to me as I read through the Old Testament, and I did it so that you don't have to. But I didn't want to re-create foods that were served at the times of the Bible, because that wasn't something that my husband or my five kids would eat. I wanted to find a way to make the Bible relevant to the modern kitchen. In my notebook I didn't just make a note every time an item of food was mentioned in the Bible, I wrote down concepts and ideas that could easily be applied to the modern kitchen. I wanted to cook and bake the way I normally do, using delicious, healthy, often kid-friendly recipes, but make the recipes into objects for table discussion. I wanted to bring the Bible into my meals in a way that would be fun, informative, and interesting, but also tasty.

Eating the Bible is truly unlike any other cookbook you've ever used. While most cookbooks offer anecdotes about a recipe, this cookbook offers serious consideration of biblical texts, which will hopefully get you thinking, while at the same time giving you "food for thought" to share with your family that relates directly to the item of food that you are serving. Unlike other cookbooks, I don't really care if you make my recipes or not (though I think you should because they are all quite yummy)— my goal in writing this cookbook was so much more than just recipes. My goal is to help you bring the Bible into your modern meals and your busy lives. This cookbook is versatile and modular: it can be experienced in-depth, providing the cook with reading material while making each recipe, which can then be imparted to family and guests, but there are also shortcuts in the form of "Alternatives" and "Questions" at the end of each recipe—quick and easy ideas to help you to bring the Bible to your table, no matter how pressed you are for time.

Alternatives—Simple, often no-bake ideas, which will enable you to discuss the same concepts at your meal as mentioned in the in-depth commentary on the recipe. Even if you don't have time to make the full recipe, the alternatives can provide either child-friendly ideas to make alongside the recipe or they can serve as

jumping-off points and inspiration for recipes of your own.

Questions—Simple questions which you can ask at your table, which directly relate to the biblical commentary. If you wish, you can use them to spark discussion and open the conversation up for you to share what you read about the recipe and the corresponding chapter of the Bible. But feel free to disregard them altogether—make each recipe your own!

The Verses and Commentary

Most of the commentary on the various verses and chapters of the Bible began simply. I read the original text in both Hebrew and English, and I stopped when I came across ideas or concepts that stumped me or because there was something there that made me think of food. Sometimes, I had my own ways of interpreting the verse and its meaning; other times I would look up the verse and see if there were parallels in other books of the Old Testament like the earlier and later prophets and writings. But sometimes I would look up words and terms in a Bible Concordance, which at times led me to the Babylonian and Jerusalem Talmud, and often to various Medieval, Renaissance, and modern commentators on those verses. Often the same things that troubled me also troubled the many scholars who had pored over the same texts at different times throughout history, and who came to sometimes similar and sometimes different conclusions. By nature, many of these sources were Jewish sources, because there is a strong tradition of biblical commentary and interpretation in Judaism. But because this is a cookbook and not a scholarly work, I do not refer to these commentators by name. That said, every source that I mention in this cookbook has been checked and verified by scholars much more knowledgeable than me, and if you would like to know the specific source for any commentary that I refer to in this cookbook, please feel free to contact me, and I will be happy to share the sources with you.

EATING THE BIBLE

Genesis

A Tree of Life

And the woman saw that the tree was good to eat, and it was a desire for the eyes, and that the tree could pleasantly make one wise, and she took of its fruit, and she ate, and she gave to her husband who was with her, and he ate.

Genesis 3:6

The Bible tells us that when God created the world, the tree was created as the symbol of life and death, of good and evil. Humankind is likened to a tree, yet God never tells us precisely which tree is the tree of life. Many have tried to figure out this quandary, but no one has come up with a conclusive answer.

Of course the apple has become the fruit we most commonly associate with this tree, but there are a few other conjectures: grapes, based on the verse "Their grapes are grapes of gall, they have clusters of bitterness" (Deuteronomy 32:32); citron, because it says, "And when the woman saw that the tree was good for food, and that it was a delight to the eyes, and a tree to be desired to make one wise" (Genesis 3:6); figs, because it says, "they sewed fig leaves together" (Genesis 3:7); and wheat, because it says in the Babylonian Talmud that a baby does not have knowledge until it can call its mother and father by name, and that a baby does not know its parents' names until it can first taste the taste of grain. Another interpretation is that the Hebrew word *chet*, which means sin, is like the word *chitah*, which means wheat.

The suggestion that the tree was a fig tree makes sense in light of the fact that Adam and Eve cover themselves with fig leaves when they "discover" that they are naked in the aftermath of their sin.

There is something very intriguing about the fact that a tree was chosen as the life-form that would serve as an example for all mankind. One of the first things God does in the Garden of Eden is plant trees. So perhaps it really doesn't matter what kind of tree it was that God planted; perhaps God wants to keep us guessing. Perhaps God wants us simply to follow in his footsteps and plant trees too; perhaps the more trees we plant, the more we learn how to take care of the trees, and the more we will learn to emulate God, no matter what type of tree it is we plant.

Garden of Eden Salad

1 cup (240 g) bulgur or wheat kernels
2 cups of water
1 Tbsp. olive oil
1 onion, chopped
1 cup (240 g) fresh mushrooms, chopped
1 tsp. dried thyme leaves
½ tsp. cinnamon
½ cup (120 g) pecans, chopped
½ cup (120 g) raisins
½ cup (120 g) dried figs, chopped
1 tsp. lemon or citron zest
Juice of half a lemon
Salt and pepper, to taste

Place 1 cup of bulgur or wheat kernels in a pot with 2 cups of water and bring to a boil. Reduce to a simmer and cook until grain is soft. Drain or add more water accordingly. Sauté onion in olive oil in a separate pan until translucent, add mushrooms and sauté 2 minutes more. Add thyme and cinnamon. Mix onion and mushroom mixture together with bulgur or wheat, add pecans, raisins, figs and citron/lemon zest. Season with lemon juice, salt and pepper.

Serves 4–6.

ALTERNATIVES:
Candied citron or lemon slices or citron or lemon jam, dried figs or fig bars, fresh grapes, raisins, wine or grape juice, or anything made from wheat—bread, cookies, cake, or pasta.

QUESTIONS: What type of fruit tree was this? Why wouldn't God have wanted to reveal the name of the tree? Why do you think Eve gave the fruit to her husband, Adam, to eat as well? Why wasn't she just content to eat the fruit herself?

Towering Contradictions

And they said: "Let us build ourselves a city and a tower whose head will be in the heavens, and we shall make a name for ourselves: lest we be scattered upon all the face of the earth."

Genesis 11:4

The generation that survived the Noahide flood decides to build a tower. They are a growing people, slowly repopulating the world after the decimation that the flood caused. They want to build a city and a tower—to begin to put down roots, set up some infrastructure. They fear dispersion, and so they want to band together and create a community. At face value there seems to be nothing wrong with that. So why does God react in this way?

One commentator explains that the tower was supposed to be a place for idol worship. Another claims that the problem was not the tower, or idol worship, but rather the fact that the people wanted to make a name for themselves. God commanded them to "be fruitful and multiply and fill the earth" (Genesis 1:28), and they wanted fame and glory instead. Still another commentator thinks that the problem was the community itself. The people of that generation aspired to create a community—to build together, to live together, to make a name for themselves as a community—to the exclusion of everything else, even God.

Other commentators see the act of building the tower not as a communal act, but as a materialistic one. They explain that the tower represented a desire to possess objects, the beginning of private property. God wants humans to live off the land, to be sustained by nature. As we see later time and again, God finds his vision of an ideal man in the simple shepherd, in Abraham, Isaac, Jacob, Joseph, Moses, and others who had time for spirituality, time to think, and time to pray to God. The generation of Babel was not God's model civilization, because they were not content to subsist on what God had provided for them, but felt a need to build, to create, to own, and to band together.

Whether the tower represented idol worship, an attempt at fame and glory, a focus on communal living to the exclusion of God, or abject materialism, God makes it clear that this is not a model on which to craft a society. It is a good lesson to us all that living a more laid-back existence, subsisting on the good that the land provides us, and consequently having time to contemplate God, is not such a bad thing at all.

Babel Vegetable Towers

2 medium-sized eggplants
4 thick zucchini
2 large sweet potatoes
3 red bell peppers
Olive oil
Salt and pepper
Dried or fresh parsley (for garnish)

Preheat oven to 400°F (200°C).

Slice eggplant, zucchini, and sweet potatoes into thick, equally sized rounds (about ¾ of an inch or 2 cm thick). Slice away the sides of the red pepper so that you have four large pieces. Sprinkle eggplant pieces with salt on both sides and let drain on paper towels for about 15 minutes. Rinse and pat dry. Place between a quarter and a third of the vegetables on a greased cookie sheet in one layer, brush lightly with olive oil, and sprinkle with salt and pepper. Place in oven and let cook for about 10 minutes. Flip vegetables and brush the other side with olive oil. Bake 5 more minutes or until soft. It will take 3–4 batches to roast all the vegetables. Once all vegetables are roasted, stack them in the following order: first the red pepper, then eggplant, then sweet potato, and last, zucchini. Dust the tops of the towers with parsley before serving.

Makes 8–10 vegetable towers.

ALTERNATIVES: Challenge your guests to see who can build a higher tower out of cookies (wafers are great!), pretzels, slices of fruit, or anything else you can stack. Confuse your guests by serving a multicultural meal—food with interesting names derived from other languages/cultures: nachos, baguettes, sauerkraut, borscht, sushi, eggrolls, goulash, samosas, falafel, and so on.

QUESTIONS: Why do you think that the people in this chapter of the Bible specifically decide to build a tower and not some other structure? Why did God punish them in the way that he did (that they should all speak different languages)? Why did they fear being scattered over the face of the earth?

Eternal Dust

And I will make your progeny like the dust of the earth: so that if a man could count the dust of the earth, then your progeny could also be counted.

Genesis 13:16

Throughout the Bible, the Israelites are compared to various innumerable inanimate objects—the dust of the earth, grains of sand, and the stars in the sky. It is easy to understand why they would be compared to the stars in the sky—who wouldn't want to be compared to a shining star? Perhaps it is also easy to understand why they would be compared to grains of sand, but why would it be considered a compliment to be compared to dust? Dust is insignificant, it is a nuisance, and it is almost intangible.

But if we examine the significance of dust, we can turn its negative qualities into positive ones. Just like dust goes from one end of the earth to other, so too will the Israelites be scattered all over the world. Just like dust can grow things only with water, so too, the Israelites can only grow with the blessing of the Bible which is compared to water, and just as the things that dust settles on can erode while the dust itself remains, so too the Israelites endure.

A bit later on in the verses, Abraham complains to God, "Behold you have not given me children" (Genesis 15:3). This is a strange comment, seeing as how God just recently promised Abraham that his offspring would be like the dust of the earth. God responds and says, "Look now toward heaven and count the stars, if you can count them . . . so shall thy seed be" (Genesis 15:5).

On the other hand, it's possible that this exchange proves that the "dust of the earth" metaphor can be understood negatively. When God responds with a new metaphor, of stars in the sky, it is actually a refinement of God's previous statement about dust. The children of Abraham will be those who will attain stardom, but they will also possess the positive character trait of humility—represented by dust.

Earthy Seasoning

1 Tbsp. paprika
1 Tbsp. salt
1 Tbsp. dry mustard
½ tsp. chili powder
1 Tbsp. cumin
2 tsp. black pepper
1 Tbsp. garlic powder
½ tsp. cayenne pepper
1 Tbsp. sugar

Mix all ingredients together and store in a tightly covered container. "Dust" onto chicken, then bake. Also great on fish, steak, and other meats!

ALTERNATIVES: Dust your table or the perimeter of each serving plate with cinnamon or other spices. Serve dipping bowls of spices that people can dip their bread into or use to season their food: garlic powder, cinnamon, salt, pepper, paprika, and cumin are all good choices.

QUESTIONS: Why dust? Yes, the dust of the earth is plentiful, but what else is so special about it?

Salty Sacrifice

And his wife looked back, behind him, and she became a pillar of salt.
Genesis 19:26

One of the most vivid and unusual episodes in the Bible is found in chapter 19 of Genesis. After attempting to save the city of Sodom from destruction, Abraham and his family flee from the city. They are all given explicit instructions not to look back. Lot's wife can't resist the temptation to catch a glimpse of the destruction, and as punishment she is turned into a pillar of salt. Why salt?

It's often explained that Lot's wife's punishment was exacted in retribution for her inhospitable actions. When the angels visited Lot, rather than welcome her guests with open arms—or at least keep their visit a secret—she acted like the rest of the people of Sodom, infamous for their unfriendly attitude toward visitors. She went to her neighbors and asked to borrow salt for her guests, so that everyone would know of their presence.

While Lot's wife was punished for having looked back to witness the destruction, her manner of death is interesting in that it preserved her for all time. In that respect, it was in some ways a legacy that she was granted. Perhaps she looked back at Sodom out of concern for her loved ones, and therefore God preserved her for eternity, despite her previous display of utter disdain for Lot's guests.

Salt-Encrusted Potatoes

4.5 lb. (2 kg) baby potatoes (a mix of red and yellow is nice)
8–10 cloves garlic, peeled
2 egg whites
2 cups (480 g) kosher salt

Preheat oven to 400°F (200°C).

    Scrub potatoes clean and dry well. Spray small baking dish with non-stick spray. Place potatoes in baking dish and distribute peeled garlic cloves. In a separate bowl, mix egg whites with salt and pour on top of potatoes to cover. Pack the salt in tight. Bake for about an hour. Let rest 15 minutes before serving. At the table, crack open the crust. Remove potatoes from the dish, dust off and enjoy! The potatoes do not taste salty—rather, the salt seals them in and bakes a moist, creamy, perfect potato.

Serves 8–10.

ALTERNATIVES: Place an extra dish of coarse or "kosher" salt at the table. Serve salty things like sardines, feta cheese, potato chips, peanuts, cold cuts, hot dogs, pickles, olives, saltine crackers, etc.

QUESTIONS: Why do you think that Lot's wife was turned into a pillar of salt? Salt is also known to be a preservative—can you think of a reason God might have wanted to preserve Lot's wife? What would have been a better punishment for Lot's wife in your opinion? Why?

Well Plotted

And afterwards, Abraham buried his wife Sarah in the cave of the field of Machpela, facing Mamre, which is Hebron, in the land of Canaan. And the field and the cave within it were established to Abraham as burial property, purchased from the sons of Chet.

Genesis 23:19-20

These verses complete what is one of the most long-winded passages in the Bible: the story of the purchase of the Machpelah cave. One commentator explains that the repetition is to call attention to the fact that the plot of land and the cave became the uncontested possession of Abraham and his family.

Another commentator asserts that the story was included both to ensure that the land of Israel would be confirmed as Abraham's inheritance, but also to stress the land's superiority above all other lands for both the living and the dead. This is the beginning of the people's physical connection to the land.

But this can even go a bit deeper, explains another commentator who sees the purchase not only as proof of possession, but as a major statement about the Israelites and their connection to the land. The fact that Abraham's first real possession is a pair of graves and a burial mound where many future generations could be buried, is as important a statement about the importance and centrality of family.

In addition, Sarah was an equal part of the plan to purchase the field of Machpelah and then be buried there. Abraham and Sarah were partners both in ensuring the importance of family and in connecting the

Israelites to the land of Israel for all time. They wanted to ensure that in the future, the land would not just be inhabited by the Israelites, but inherited.

Fudge Cave Cake

1½ cups (340 g) butter or margarine, softened
1½ cups (300 g) sugar
6 eggs
2 cups (250 g) powdered sugar
2 cups (250 g) flour
¾ cup (95 g) cocoa powder
1½ cups (360 g) walnuts, chopped

Glaze (optional)
¾ cup (95 g) powdered sugar
¼ cup (30 g) cocoa powder
1½–2 Tbsp. milk (or nondairy creamer, soy milk, or water)

Preheat oven to 350°F (180°C). Grease a Bundt or tube pan.

Beat butter or margarine and regular sugar in large bowl with an electric mixer until light and fluffy. Add eggs, one at a time, beating well after each addition. Gradually add powdered sugar, blending well. By hand, stir in flour, cocoa, and walnuts until well blended.

Spoon batter into pan. Bake for 50 minutes. Cool in pan for 1 hour. Invert onto serving plate. Cool completely. Combine glaze ingredients and spoon over top of cake. Serve.

Serves 10–12.

ALTERNATIVES: Serve chocolate coins for dessert. Purchase and serve cookies that look like little mountains (like Mallows or Mallomars). Purchase and serve a chocolate jelly roll cake or mounded cake to represent the cave.

QUESTIONS: Why was it so important to Abraham to own a plot of land for the burial of his wife? Why didn't he want to own a plot of land before this? Why was this plot of land a cave?

The Pot Simmers

And Esau said to Jacob, "Please give some of this red, red stew,
for I am faint"; and he was therefore named Edom.

Genesis 25:30

There is much confusion and many questions that
come out of the series of verses that describe Jacob's
"purchase" of Esau's birthright for the infamous
"mess of pottage." The first question that comes to my
mind is why was Jacob cooking lentil soup, and why
did the Bible feel a need to tell us about his culinary
experiments in the kitchen?

One commentator answers this question very
practically, stating that Abraham had died on that day
and Jacob was cooking lentils to feed the mourners.
Furthermore, Jacob was cooking lentils because he
understood their significance—since they are round,
like a wheel, they help to remind a mourner that life
goes on. And because they have no mouth (no crack) like
other beans, they help remind the mourner that he does
not have to speak, as a mourner often does not respond
to anyone's greetings for the first few days of mourning.

Esau comes along and demands to eat some "red
stuff." As another commentator explains, he is so tired
he cannot even recognize what it is that Jacob is cooking
nor its symbolism. Jacob is so upset by what he takes as
Esau's lack of awareness that Abraham has died that he
decides that Esau does not deserve the birthright.

When Jacob asks Esau for the birthright, Esau
says to Jacob, "I am going to die anyway; so why do
I need this birthright?"(Genesis 25:32) It is said in
the Babylonian Talmud that Esau was exhausted
because he had transgressed five cardinal sins that day:

adultery, murder, heresy, denial of the resurrection and despising the birthright. Commentators even suggest that God shortened Abraham's life by five years so that he would die on that day and be spared the vision of Esau sinning. After all of the sinning he had engaged in, including a complete denial of God, Esau knew he would die and so the birthright meant nothing to him.

One commentator opines that before Esau handed over the birthright, he asked Jacob what it entailed. When Jacob explained the Temple service and the prohibitions associated with the birthright, Esau thought that the birthright would literally kill him, for he would not be able to keep all the commandments associated with it.

Perhaps this chapter of the Bible is the source for the dictum "you are what you eat." Red lentils, when cooked long enough, normally turn pink and then yellow when cooked properly—and it doesn't even take very long for the color change to occur. The fact that the lentils were still red means that they were basically raw (as evidenced by the use of the Hebrew word *na*, which could mean "please," but as in Exodus 12:9, can also mean "raw.") Esau becomes Edom (from the Hebrew word *adom*— "red") because he cannot control his physical desires long enough to even allow a pot of red lentils to cook.

Red Lentil Soup

1 large onion, chopped

3 cloves garlic, crushed

2 Tbsp. olive oil

2 tsp. cumin

1 tsp. ground coriander

1 Tbsp. paprika

2 tsp. salt

½ tsp. pepper

2 cups (480 g) red lentils

8–10 cups (1900–2400 mL) chicken stock or water

Juice of ½–1 lemon

Sauté onion and garlic in olive oil until translucent. Add cumin, coriander, paprika, salt, and pepper, and cook 1–2 minutes more. Add lentils and cook 1–2 minutes more. Add stock or water and let simmer for half an hour, adding more water as needed to obtain desired consistency. This is a thick soup in general. Stir in lemon juice and adjust seasoning to taste.

Serves 8–10.

ALTERNATIVES: Add red lentils to a stew, serve a red lentil salad or mujadara (rice and lentils). You could also serve other red foods—red peppers, tomatoes, strawberries, red Jell-O, tomato sauce, red meat, and so on. Or "twin" foods like sandwich cookies, two serving plates of every food you've made, or give everyone two forks, two plates, two cups, etc.

QUESTIONS: Why did Esau think that he was about to die? Why do you think he calls the food that Jacob is cooking "red" twice? Why does the Bible then make the point of telling us that it is because of this request of his (or this incident) that he is called "Edom"?

Magical Mandrakes

And Reuben went in the days of the wheat harvest, and he found dudaim in the field and he brought them to Leah, his mother. And Rachel said to Leah, "Please give me some of your son's dudaim." And she said to her, "Isn't it enough that you have taken my husband, now you wish also to take my son's dudaim?" So Rachel said, "Therefore, he shall sleep with you tonight in return for your son's dudaim." And Jacob came from the field in the evening, and Leah went out to him, and said, "You shall come to me, because I rented you with my son's dudaim," and he slept with her on that night.

Genesis 30:14-16

Though the word *dudaim* is generally translated as mandrake, a plant notorious for its narcotic and aphrodisiac properties, commentators are at odds over precisely what type of flower these dudaim were. The word appears again in the Song of Songs (7:14), where it says that dudaim have a pleasant aroma. One commentator renders the word as jasmine, while in Jeremiah (24:1) it is a reference to two baskets of figs. In other sources, dudaim are either mandrakes, violets, or barley.

The nature of the dudaim plant is significant, if only to understand what this incident is attempting to relate to us. Was this plant an aphrodisiac? A fertility drug? A mood enhancer? Or something more?

One commentator flatly dismisses the plant's medicinal properties and claims the use of the plant was merely as a good-luck charm. But the mandrake root actually does contain scopolamine and hyoscyamine, two chemical compounds that may be used as medicines or poisons. Throughout history and in literature, the mandrake root has been hailed as a magic plant, an aphrodisiac and a fertility drug, and legend has it that when the plant is pulled from the ground it shrieks in pain (as referenced in the second Harry Potter novel).

However, some commentators derive meaning for this biblical episode from the etymology of the word dudaim. The Hebrew word *dod* means a lover or a friend. Rachel had no lack of love from her husband—she was his favored wife, the one he worked fourteen years to marry—but she lacked the love that Leah had, the love of a child, for it is Reuben who went out to the field to fetch the dudaim for his mother.

Jasmine Rice with Figs

1 small onion, chopped
1 celery stalk, chopped
2 Tbsp. olive oil
1 tsp. curry powder
1 tsp. nutmeg
1 cup (240 g) jasmine rice
2 cups (475 mL) chicken stock
¼ cup (60 g) dried cranberries
¼ cup (60 g) dried figs
¼ cup (40 mL) toasted sunflower seeds
1 Tbsp. fresh mint, chopped
Salt and pepper, to taste

Brown onion and celery in oil for 2–3 minutes. Add curry powder and nutmeg, and cook 1–2 minutes more. Add jasmine rice, cook for 3 minutes longer. Pour in chicken stock, bring to a boil, and reduce heat to low. Cover and cook for 20 minutes. Take off heat and stir in dried cranberries, figs, sunflower seeds, mint, salt, and pepper.

Serves 4–6.

ALTERNATIVES: Place a pot of African violets on your table. Serve jasmine tea, jasmine rice, dried figs, fig bars, and even mandrake liqueur from Kibbutz Mishmar Ha'emek in the north of Israel, where mandrakes are grown!

QUESTIONS: What do you think these dudaim represent? Why was Reuben involved in all of this? Why do you think Rachel was so desperate to purchase these dudaim that she was willing to give up a night with her husband for the privilege or pleasure of having them?

Sealed with a Kiss

And Esau ran toward him and embraced him,
and he fell on his neck and kissed him, and they cried.
Genesis 33:4

Based on the phonetic relationship between the words *vayishakeihu* ("and he kissed him"), and *vayinashcheihu* ("and he bit him"), it has been suggested that perhaps Esau did not come to kiss Jacob, but rather to bite him. And legend even has it that Jacob's neck miraculously turned to hard marble that Esau knocked his teeth against.

Others have suggested that perhaps Esau did not kiss Jacob wholeheartedly, hence the unclear word choice, or that at that moment Esau had mercy on his brother Jacob and kissed him wholeheartedly, even though he had intended to bite him

More than anything, this peculiar incident teaches us that things are not always what they seem. It teaches us much about human nature: thirty-six years of separation is not always enough to heal a family feud, or to reunite brothers with no strings attached and no grudges borne, but if one goes about it in the right way, reconciliation is possible. On the other hand, the embrace of one's enemies, even familial ones, must still be looked upon with caution.

No matter what meaning you ascribe to Esau's kiss, here is a recipe that will spark a discussion on the subject.

Marble Pound Cake with a Hard Chocolate Crust

1½ cups (300 g) sugar

¾ cup (170 g) butter or margarine

3 cups (375 g) flour

2 tsp. baking powder

1 tsp. baking soda

1 cup (240 mL) orange juice

2 tsp. vanilla

3 eggs

½ tsp. salt

¼ cup (30 g) cocoa powder

1 cup (240 g) chocolate chips

Preheat oven to 350°F (180°C). Grease a 10-inch (25 cm) tube or Bundt pan.

Beat sugar and butter until light and fluffy.

Add remaining ingredients, except cocoa and chocolate chips, and beat until well mixed. Pour half of batter into pan. Add cocoa to remaining batter and mix well. Pour or spoon into pan over white batter and swirl with a knife to obtain marbled effect. Bake for 45–60 minutes or until toothpick inserted in center comes out clean.

Immediately after the cake comes out of the oven, pour chocolate chips over cake. Allow the chocolate chips to melt for a few minutes and then smear over entire cake with a knife. Allow the cake to cool completely, then place in fridge to harden chocolate before turning cake out onto a plate. The chocolate chips create a crust that will be difficult to cut through, but well worth the effort.

Serves 10–12.

ALTERNATIVES: Serve Hershey's Kisses, or make cookies decorated with chocolate "kisses" or hearts. Make chicken soup with a chicken or turkey neck and place the neck in a bowl on the table. Serve "bite"-sized hors d'oeuvres, or use Tabasco or other hot sauce in your cooking, to give everything at your table a little "bite."

QUESTIONS: Why do you think Esau was the one who ran to his brother? Do you think he was sincere in giving him a hug and a kiss? The verse says that both of the brothers wept—what do you think they were crying about?

True Colors

And Israel loved Joseph more than all of his sons, because he was a child of his old age; and he made him a garment of stripes (ketonet passim).

Genesis 37:3

Made famous by Andrew Lloyd Webber's musical *Joseph and the Amazing Technicolor Dreamcoat.* Joseph's *ketonet passim* is commonly rendered in many translations of the Bible as a "coat of many colors." While there are commentators who translate *passim* as colors, its literal definition is "a garment of stripes"; yet many sources debate the nature of this infamous jacket that evoked such jealousy among Joseph's brothers.

Samuel 13:18 refers to a *ketonet passim* as a royal garment worn by Tamar (King David's daughter) and all the other daughters of the king. One commentator translates the word *passim* as "length" meaning the cloak extended to Joseph's ankles.

According to another commentator, the coat was made of fine wool, but others claim the coat was made of silk, or that it was striped, embroidered, or covered with pictures. Still another commentator discusses this type of tunic as part of the attire of the priests and claims that the tunic was made of the forbidden combination of wool and linen.

Abel was a shepherd who raised sheep, which produce wool; Cain worked the land raising flax, which produces linen. Perhaps Jacob gave Joseph a coat made of wool and linen to signify the original rift in brotherly

love that was caused when Cain slew Abel. Jacob was hoping that through a garment that brought Cain and Abel back together via the meshing of wool and linen, Joseph would be inspired to heal the rift between himself and his brothers.

Technicolor Salad with Silky Avocado Dressing

1 head romaine lettuce, chopped

1 11 oz. (312 g) can mandarin orange slices

1 red pepper, sliced into thin strips

1 yellow pepper, sliced into thin strips

1 carrot, sliced thin

2 cucumbers, halved lengthwise and sliced thin

1 small red onion, sliced thin and separated into rings

1 mango, diced

1 avocado, one half diced and the other reserved for the dressing

1 cup (150 g) cashew nuts or sugared almonds

Silky Avocado Dressing

½ of reserved avocado

1 Tbsp. lemon juice

1 Tbsp. rice wine vinegar or white vinegar

1 tsp. salt

2 cloves fresh garlic, crushed

¼ cup (60 mL) water

1–2 tsp. sugar, to taste

Pinch of cayenne pepper, to taste

Place all dressing ingredients in a blender or food processor and mix until smooth, adding more water until desired consistency is achieved.

Assemble all salad ingredients in a bowl and pour on dressing just before serving.

Serves 8–10.

ALTERNATIVES: Multicolored cookies (with rainbow sprinkles) or a striped vegetable platter (slice multicolored vegetables into long strips and arrange nicely on a platter). Set the table with a richly embroidered tablecloth or use striped napkins to decorate your table. However I really must request that you not attempt to combine wool and linen at your table—unless it will heal a family feud!

QUESTIONS: What do you think Joseph's *ketonet passim* looked like? Why do you think that Jacob gave it to him? Why was Joseph dubbed "the son of his old age"—isn't Benjamin even younger?

Gifts of Contrition?

And Israel their father said to them: If it be so, then do this: take from
the best of the land in your vessels and bring the man a gift: a little balsam,
a little honey, some gum and resin, pistachios and almonds.

Genesis 43:11

When Jacob realizes that he has no other option but
to send his son Benjamin down to Egypt to meet the
demands of the disguised Joseph, now viceroy of Egypt,
he formulates a plan.

Sending presents to pacify one's enemy was a
strategy that Jacob himself employed in his meeting
with his brother Esau, only a few chapters earlier. One
commentator explains his rationale thus: If you bring
gifts to someone who is impressed by wealth, it must be
plentiful enough to satisfy that desire, as was Jacob's
gift to Esau. However, if you send a gift to someone
not impressed by wealth, it is better that it is smaller
in quantity, but of a quality that would be appreciated
even in the king's palace. Such was the offering brought
to Joseph.

Though there is some disagreement between the
commentators as to the identity of some of the products
that were sent to Joseph, there is no disputing the use
of three of the same Hebrew words in the account of the
sale of Joseph.

This offering that the brothers brought to Joseph
had a double purpose. From a practical standpoint these
items were chosen to represent the produce of the land
of Israel (instead of the more typical seven species since
it was a time of famine). These items were not available
in Egypt and are not drastically affected by famine. Yet

they may have also served a more symbolic purpose: at once a care package from home, a reminder of betrayal, and an offering of forgiveness.

And indeed, after receiving these gifts from his native land, Joseph immediately asks about his father, and upon seeing Benjamin is so overcome with emotion that he hurries out of the room to compose himself (Genesis 43:25–30). The brothers, through the offering of these unusual gifts, have brought their relationship with Joseph full circle.

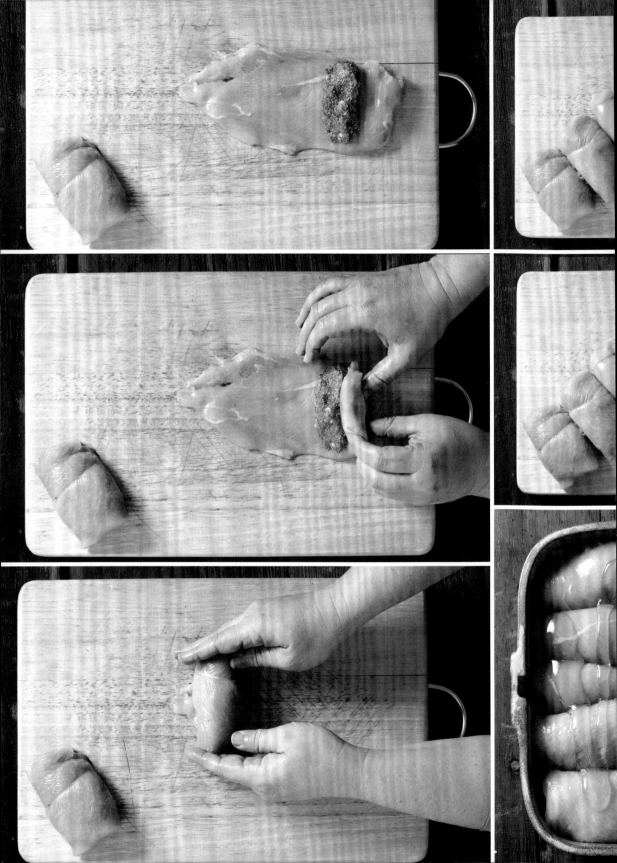

Pistachio Almond Chicken Parcels

½ cup (120 g) breadcrumbs
½ cup (130 g) toasted and ground pistachio nuts
½ cup (130 g) toasted and ground almonds
1 tsp. cinnamon
½ tsp. nutmeg
½ tsp. salt
½ tsp. pepper
1 cup (240 ml) honey
6 skinless, boneless chicken breasts, pounded thin
    (about 2 lb. or 1 kg)

Preheat oven to 350°F (180°C).

In a bowl, combine breadcrumbs, pistachio nuts, almonds, cinnamon, nutmeg, salt, pepper, and ½ cup honey. Mix. Place 1–2 Tbsp. of nut mixture in the center of each chicken breast, roll up and place in a greased baking dish.

Drizzle remaining honey over the chicken, sprinkle remaining nut mixture over chicken (if some remains) and bake for 25–30 minutes or until center of parcel is no longer pink. (It is worth starting to check after 20 minutes.) Drizzle lightly with more honey before serving.

Serves 6.

ALTERNATIVES: Serve pistachios, almonds, almond cookies, marzipan, or make or buy a honey cake. Serve honey with tea, offer gum instead of an after-dinner mint, or give a gift of sugared almonds, roasted pistachio nuts, and honey to your guests or your hosts.

QUESTIONS: Why do you think that Jacob felt a need to send gifts with Benjamin at all? Why did they choose such an unusual assortment of goods? Why did the Bible feel it important to tell us exactly the gifts that they brought?

The Wheels Are Turning

And to his father he sent the following: ten donkeys laden with the best of Egypt's products, and ten female donkeys laden with grain, bread and food for his father's journey.

Genesis 45:23

And when they told him everything that Joseph said to them and he saw the wagons that Joseph sent to transport him, the spirit of Jacob their father was revived.

Genesis 45:27

At first glance, these six verses read as a very practical narrative. Joseph sends wagons (at the request of Pharaoh) to collect his father. He also sends donkeys, provisions, and gifts—a fitting tribute to a long-lost parent from a viceroy of Egypt. But Jacob's enthusiastic response instructs us to dig a little deeper. Why would Jacob's spirit be revived at the sight of the wagons?

The commentators all agree that Joseph was sending a coded message to his father. According to the Babylonian Talmud "Egypt's finest product" was aged wine and Joseph sent this to his father to comfort him. Just as wine improves with age and gains value, so too had Jacob improved with age in the twenty-two years that they had been apart.

Another commentator explains a different aspect of this coded message. Joseph sent ten donkeys to hint to his father that he did not blame his brothers for what happened. His brothers were like donkeys that carried their load blindly. They were acting according to God's plan when they sold Joseph; they were merely pawns in the process.

But the wagons are what really impress Jacob. Apparently, the sign Joseph sent (via Pharaoh) through the wagons served to remind Jacob of the last subject that they had studied together before they were separated. According to this commentator, it was the chapter on *egla arufa*—the calf whose neck is broken to expiate the sin of an unsolved murder and absolve the surrounding cities of guilt (Deuteronomy 21). The root letters of the word *egla* (calf) are similar to *agala* (wagon), and in this way Joseph told his father that he did not forget anything that he had taught him, despite his long sojourn in Egypt. Moreover, just as the calf's neck is broken in lieu of punishing the unknown murderer, Joseph was absolving his father and brothers of any guilt they may feel and the hesitation they might have in coming to join him in Egypt.

Wagon Wheel Pasta Salad

1 lb. (454 g) bag or box wheel shaped pasta
1 red pepper, chopped
1 tomato, chopped
1 avocado, diced
1 15 oz. (425 g) can black beans, drained and rinsed
1 10 oz. (283 g) can corn, drained
1–2 cloves garlic, crushed
2 Tbsp. fresh cilantro, chopped
Juice of ½ lemon
½ tsp. cumin
½–1 tsp. chili powder, or a few drops of Tabasco sauce
    (to taste)
Salt and pepper, to taste

In a large bowl, combine the red pepper, tomato, avocado, black beans, corn, garlic, and cilantro. Stir in the lemon juice, cumin, and chili powder or Tabasco sauce. Let sit for half an hour to allow the flavors to combine.

Before serving, place cooked pasta in a serving bowl and add the vegetable mixture. Add salt and pepper to taste. (If serving dairy, you can add a dollop of sour cream or a sprinkle of shredded cheese to each portion.)
Serves 4—6.

ALTERNATIVES: Arrange slices of citrus, avocado, red bell pepper, or other vegetables on a plate in the shape of a wagon wheel. Make little wagons out of celery, carrots, peanut butter, and raisins (cut a small section of celery, fill with peanut butter, use two round carrot slices for wheels, and decorate with raisins). Serve round cookies for dessert, and don't forget some good-quality aged wine!

QUESTIONS: Why do you think that Joseph sent wagons to his father instead of going himself? Why do you think that Jacob's spirit was revived at the sight of the wagons?

Fishy Business

May the angel who redeems me from all harm bless the youths,
and may they be called by my name and the name of my fathers, Abraham and Isaac,
and may they multiply like fish, in the midst of the land.
Genesis 48:16

On his deathbed, Jacob blesses his grandchildren, Joseph's children, Ephraim and Manasseh. Almost every other time that a quantitative blessing is given in the Bible the content usually invokes the stars or grains of sand as a blessing for the exponential increase of one's descendants. But here, Joseph's sons are blessed to increase like fish.

What is it about fish that is so blessed?

One commentator explains that fish, which proliferate and multiply, are unaffected by the evil eye—the power (real or imagined) that someone might have to cause you bad luck or injury by looking at you with an ill-meaning glance. This would explain why fish are a common sign for luck and protection in the Middle East. The symbol of the fish often appears together with the hamsa hand and other good luck symbols.

But this is problematic. Does this mean that the evil eye cannot penetrate water? What's more, the blessing stipulates that Ephraim and Manasseh "will increase in the midst of the land like fish," but fish cannot live out of water.

Another commentator explains this seeming contradiction. This blessing connects Joseph's sons, their descendents, and fish at a much deeper level. Just as fish live their lives oblivious to the eyes of

humans, the descendants of Jacob will lead their lives "in the midst of the land," able to go about their lives unaffected by their surroundings.

Joseph's sons Ephraim and Manasseh embody that blessing because they were born and raised in Egypt, but were nonetheless accorded equal status with the rest of Jacob's children (their uncles) who were not raised in a foreign land.

Rice Blessed with Arrabbiata-Style Fish

4½ lb. (2 kg) halibut, cod, or sole fillets (fresh or frozen)
Salt and pepper
Juice of 1 lemon
1 onion, chopped
2 cloves garlic, crushed
2 Tbsp. olive oil
½ tsp. red pepper flakes (or to taste)
½ cup (120 mL) white wine
1 15 oz. (425 g) can crushed tomatoes
1 Tbsp. sugar
2 Tbsp. minced fresh parsley
1 Tbsp. minced fresh basil
2 cups rice (400 g)

Place fish in a large baking dish and sprinkle with salt, pepper, and lemon juice. Allow to sit about 15 minutes.

In the meantime, in a deep pan, sauté onion and garlic in olive oil for 5 minutes. Add red pepper flakes and wine, and cook for 1 minute. Add tomatoes, bring to a boil, and stir in sugar, parsley, and basil. Cut fish into large chunks and add to sauce. Cook on low to medium flame 15–20 minutes, until fish is cooked through. In the meantime, cook the 2 cups of rice.

Serve fish on a bed of rice.

Serves 8–10.

ALTERNATIVES: Fish! Tuna quiche, salmon concealed in puff pastry or phyllo dough, Angel Food Cake. Set your table with hamsas, scatter turquoise beads and eye charms, or tie napkins with red string.

QUESTIONS: Why do you think it is a blessing to increase like the fish of the sea? Why are the Israelites compared to fish? Why do you think that we sing this song to little children? Who is the angel that is mentioned in the verse?

Exodus

Mortar and Memories

And they embittered their lives with hard labor,
with mortar and with bricks and with all kinds of labor in the fields,
in all of their work they worked with back-breaking labor.

Exodus 1:14

The commentators ask why the verse "mortar and bricks" is singled out and not subsumed under the more general statement of "hard labor," and "all kinds of labor in the field." It is suggested that the work done by the Israelites in Egypt with mortar and bricks was the beginning of all the other labor.

This makes sense in hindsight. Today, when we think of the hard work that the Israelites performed as slaves in Egypt, we tend to envision the building of pyramids—work involving bricks and mortar. Indeed, one of the most tasty food items at the Passover Seder is the *charoset*—a mixture of apples, nuts, wine, and cinnamon concocted to replicate mortar.

The Jastrow Talmudic Dictionary parses the word charoset as coming from the Hebrew root *cheres,* meaning earthenware, which is made with clay, or in the case of bricklaying, mortar.

The common suggestion is that charoset is eaten at the Passover Seder in memory of the mortar the Israelites used to build with, but one commentator suggests that apples are a main ingredient in the

charoset in tribute to the Israelite women who gave birth under apple or citrus trees in Egypt so that they might hide their baby boys and shield them from Pharaoh's infanticide decree. If we follow in the spirit of this opinion, charoset is a symbol of hope. Charoset is eaten on Passover to remember that despite the backbreaking labor, there was still hope.

Brick-Shaped Turkey Meatloaf with Cranberry Charoset

1 onion, finely chopped
2–3 cloves garlic, crushed
1 Tbsp. olive oil
1 carrot, finely chopped
1 cup (240 g) mushrooms, finely chopped
1 tsp. salt
½ tsp. pepper
2 Tbsp. fresh parsley, chopped
2¼ lb. (1 kg) ground turkey
1 cup (200 g) breadcrumbs
3 Tbsp. ketchup
2 eggs

Preheat oven to 350ºF (180°C).

Sauté onion and garlic in oil until onion is soft, 3–5 minutes. Add carrot and cook 5 more minutes. Add mushrooms, salt, and pepper, and cook 5 more minutes. Stir in parsley and set aside.

Stir together ground turkey, breadcrumbs, ketchup, and eggs; then add vegetable mixture.

Form into a brick either by using a loaf pan or by molding the brick with your hands in a greased baking dish. Spread with additional ketchup and bake for 45 minutes.

Serves 4–6.

Cranberry Sauce (Charoset)
1 15 oz. (425 g) can whole berry cranberry sauce
2 cups (480 g) coarsely chopped apples
½ cup (120 g) chopped walnuts
½ cup (120 mL) orange juice
¼ cup (60 mL) sweet red wine
1 tsp. cinnamon
Sugar, to taste

Combine all ingredients in a bowl and refrigerate.

TO SERVE: Cut one slice of meatloaf, then cut it in half. Spread the charoset as the mortar between the two halves, then sandwich them together again (as pictured). Serve extra sauce on the side.

ALTERNATIVES: Use peanut butter, apple butter, caramel spread, chocolate spread, or any other thick and gooey, mortar-like substance to put together cookie "bricks." Chummus or cream cheese could be used as mortar for crackers too.

QUESTIONS: What is the difference between "hard labor," work with "mortar and bricks," and "all kinds of labor in the fields"? Why does the Bible list these different types of work like this: "all the work that they worked with back breaking labor"? Ok, we get the point. They worked hard. Enough! Is it just for emphasis? Or is there something else going on here?

Plaguing the Egyptian Conscience

Because this time, I am sending all my plagues to your heart and to your servants and to your people, so that you shall know that here is none like me in all of the land.

Exodus 9:14

In verse 14, God tells Moses to tell Pharaoh that this time he is sending all of his plagues. However, God then proceeds to send the plague of hail. One commentator explains that here he is referring to the plague of the firstborn. But others explain that it is not the plague of the firstborn, but rather the plague of the first of the crops, which were almost completely devastated by the plague of hail. What was it about this plague that made it equivalent to all the other plagues?

One commentator opines that God refers to this plague as "all my plagues" because the type of hail sent included extremely loud thunder (or strong wind) and the miraculous combination of fire and ice, essentially a combination of all the elements. Indeed this is the first time that we see Pharaoh react in fear and even state, "God is righteous, and my nation and I are evil" (Exodus 9:27).

Another commentator explains that this plague was unique because it consisted of a miracle within a miracle: the fire and the hail were mixed together, two elements which made peace between themselves to do the will of their creator. Additionally, according to another commentator, the first plagues caused no lasting damage, whereas hail was the first plague to do permanent damage to the land. This fiery storm destroyed the flax and barley (9:31), only to be followed by the plague of locusts which destroyed whatever was

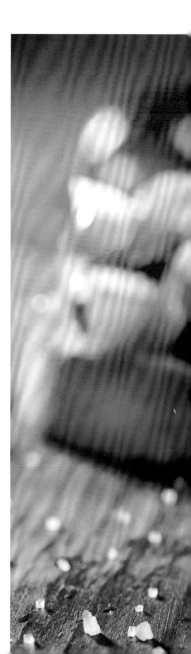

left. After these, the only plagues left were the plague of darkness and the plague of the firstborn. The plague of hail is really the beginning of the end for Pharaoh and the Egyptians.

Fire and Ice Bruschetta

6 tomatoes, diced
1 onion, chopped fine
½ cup (120 mL) vinegar
½ tsp. black pepper
2 Tbsp. sugar
⅛ tsp. cayenne pepper, or more to taste
A few drops of Tabasco sauce or 1 seeded chili pepper,
chopped very fine (optional)
1 baguette, sliced into thin rounds
Olive oil

Cut tomatoes and onions and place in a bowl with a lid. Place remaining ingredients, except for baguette and olive oil, in a saucepan and bring to boil. Immediately pour over vegetables, shake up, and chill for at least 1 hour. Brush baguette with olive oil, and toast until crisp. Serve fire and ice tomato mixture spooned on top of toasted baguette rounds.

Serves 4–6.

ALTERNATIVES: Serve ice cold drinks and red hot food. Serve any cold salad that is spicy as well. Serve Baked Alaska or fried ice cream. Sprinkle cayenne pepper on top of vanilla ice cream (it actually tastes really good!), or simply put out a bowl of ice on your table with some Tabasco sauce on the side.

QUESTIONS: What is so awe-inspiring about the mixture of fire and ice? Why do you think God chose to send a plague in the form of hail? Why didn't God just destroy all the crops?

Dark, Dark Nights

And they obscured the face of all the land, and the land became darkened.
Exodus 10:15

And Moses stretched out his hand to the sky, and there was thick darkness over the entire land of Egypt for three days.
Exodus 10:22

This chapter of the Bible is riddled with references to the dark. Commentators point out that the three plagues mentioned in this chapter are all associated with darkness. The Egyptians are first struck with a cloud of locusts so thick it blocks the sun (Exodus 10:15). Then they are hit with the plague of darkness, during which they cannot move because of all its viscosity. Finally, the plague of the firstborn strikes at the stroke of midnight.

God uses a three-pronged approach against the Egyptians here. He shows the Egyptians mastery over the winds when the locusts are blown both to and away from Egypt by strong winds. He demonstrates mastery over the sun, which the Egyptians worshipped as a god, through the plague of darkness, and he demonstrates ultimate mastery over even the womb during the plague of the firstborn.

One commentator states that the thick darkness lasted for six days. For the first three days nobody could see each other, but during the next three days the darkness became so palpable that the Egyptians were frozen in place. According to some, this was the time for the Israelites to go through the homes of the Egyptians and take back the possessions that were stolen from them.

Another commentator explains the significance of all this darkness. Night is divided into two clear parts: the first, where the darkness becomes greater and greater, and the second, when the darkness begins to lessen and fade into morning. Corresponding to its nature, the first half of the night is linked to severity or justice, while the second half is linked to mercy and benevolence. It was at the juxtaposition of severity and mercy, darkness and light, that God chose to simultaneously strike and redeem. Midnight marked both the culmination of a severe justice-rendering, ten-plague process for the Egyptians, and the dawn of a new day for the Israelites, who left the darkness of Egypt not as slaves but as wealthy men.

Hidden Treasure Midnight Brownies

¾ cup (180 g) dark chocolate
½ cup (113 g) butter or margarine
1½ cups (190 g) powdered sugar
½ cup (65 g) flour
3 large eggs
3 large egg yolks
½ cup (120 g) silver/gold sprinkles

Preheat oven to 400°F (200°C). Grease a 12-muffin tin.

Melt chocolate and butter together until smooth (either in a microwave or on stovetop). Add powdered sugar and flour. Beat eggs and egg yolks, and add to chocolate mixture. Fill muffin cups halfway, top with silver/gold sprinkles, then spoon on remaining brownie mixture. Bake 8–10 minutes or until edges are set. Centers will be soft. Cool 2 minutes. Loosen each cupcake with a knife and turn out onto a plate or cookie sheet.

Makes 12 brownies.

ALTERNATIVES: Serve brownies or any other type of dark chocolate cake, dark chocolate, or chocolate liqueur. Make sure to dim the lights and snack at midnight.

QUESTIONS: What is the difference between obscuring the view of the earth and the earth becoming darkened? Why are we informed a few verses later that "there was thick darkness"? Didn't we already know this? And if not, what is the difference between thick darkness and regular darkness?

To the Manna Born

And the house of Israel named it manna, and it was like a white coriander seed,
and its taste was like a wafer of honey.
Exodus 16:31

As children we learn that manna was the ultimate food. It was a food that changed its flavor according to your cravings and desires. And yet, the above verse tells us exactly what the manna tasted like. How is this so?

Additionally, the verse above is not the first time we see manna mentioned. The Israelites first ask for meat and bread (Exodus 16:3), God replies that he will give them meat and bread (16:12), and then proceeds to give them quail (16:13) and an unrecognizable food-like item (16:15) that they call manna. Yet we are not told what the manna resembles or tastes like until verse 31. Why were they given meat in the form of quail and bread in the form of some unidentified food item that does not even resemble bread, and why did it take them until the Sabbath to figure out what it tasted like?

The link between the Sabbath and manna is vital. Two loaves were to be gathered on the Sabbath, no other amount and at no other time. The manna was sandwiched between two layers of dew, and it was specifically on the Sabbath that the manna was supposed to taste like honey.

Manna was a gift from heaven, but it required some work to turn it into something edible. In Numbers 11:8, we see that "the people went about and gathered it, and ground it in mills, or crushed it in a mortar, and simmered it in pots, and made cakes of it; and the taste of it was as the taste of a cake baked with oil." In this way it resembled bread. God was prepared to send

quail, but bread he was not willing to make fall from the sky. It was only when the Israelites worked extra hard and gathered and prepared a double recipe of bread for the Sabbath ahead of time, that they were able to kick back and relax enough to properly appreciate and savor manna's sweet qualities.

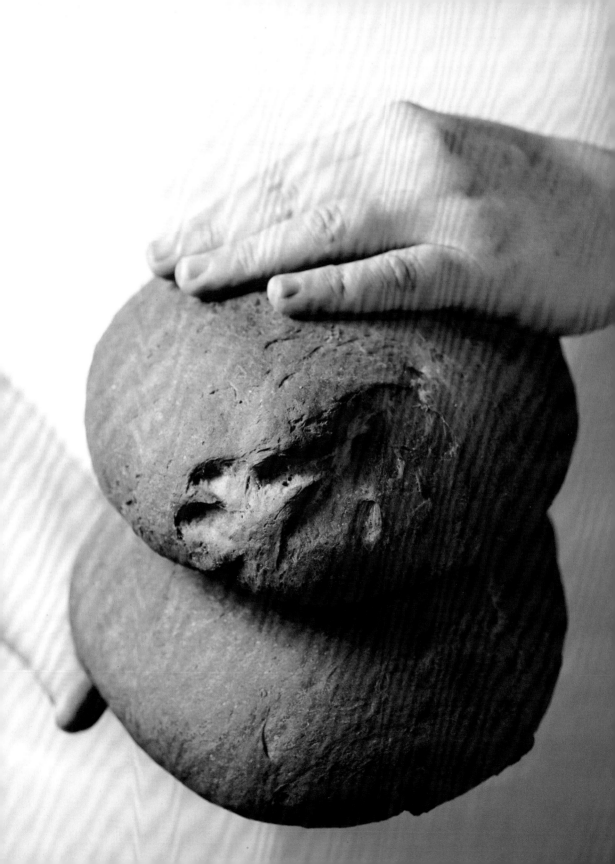

Honey Coriander Manna Bread

1 cup (240 mL) lukewarm water
Pinch of sugar
1 Tbsp. active dry yeast
½ cup (120 mL) honey
1 egg
½ cup (113 g) butter or margarine, melted
1 Tbsp. ground coriander
1½ tsp. salt
½ tsp. ground cinnamon
¼ tsp. ground cloves
¼ tsp. ground ginger
1 Tbsp. grated orange zest (optional)
4–5 cups flour (500 g–625 g) (you can use half whole
   wheat)

Combine lukewarm water, sugar, and yeast. Allow to sit for about 5 minutes until yeast is frothy. Add rest of ingredients except flour. Stir in the flour 1 cup at a time. Knead until dough is smooth and elastic. Place in a large, greased bowl, wrap entire bowl in a plastic bag or cover with a dishtowel, and allow to rise for 1½ hours or until dough has doubled in size.

Punch down dough and knead again. Generously grease two baking sheets or loaf pans with butter or margarine and place the loaves in the pans or on the baking sheets.

Preheat oven to 350°F (180°C).

Cover bread with a tea towel and allow dough to rise until doubled in bulk, 45–60 minutes. Bake for 30–40 minutes or until golden brown.

Each loaf serves 4–6.

If serving on the Sabbath make sure to make a double portion!

ALTERNATIVES: Use coriander to spice up your food in any recipe, add cilantro (the leaves of the coriander plant) to your salad, serve tofu or any other bland white food that resembles manna. You can serve honey-glazed doughnuts for dessert!

QUESTIONS: What was manna? Why was it called by that name? What types of food do we eat that resemble or remind you of manna? If you could eat something that tasted every day like something else what would it be? What texture would it have? How do you eat differently on the weekends? What is your double portion?

Clouds of Obscurity

And the nation stood from afar, but Moses approached the thick cloud, where God was.
Exodus 20:17

We are told that God appears under the cover of a thick cloud three times in chapter 20 of Exodus. Even one mention would be enough to prompt the question: why did God need to mask himself in the gloom of a cloud? Here, at the revelation of Sinai, when God reveals himself to the Israelites, when they are given the Ten Commandments, when we are told that all of the people saw and heard God, here God shrouds himself in a cloud? It makes no sense.

One commentator explains that the cloud was there to decrease visibility so that the people's sense of hearing would be more acute, as it says in Exodus 19:9, "in order that the people may hear when I speak." Yet at the same time we are told that "All the people saw the voices" (Exodus 20:15) and that "God will come down on Mount Sinai before the eyes of all the people" (Exodus 19:11).

Indeed, another commentator explains that even Moses must wade through three barriers—darkness, cloud, and fog—when he approaches Mount Sinai. So what did everyone see?

Still another commentator explains that the reason God appeared in the thickness of cloud was because he wanted the Israelites to emulate him, to be a source of light amidst the darkness of the world. The people saw the thick cloud, but they had no doubt that God (in the form of light) was hidden within the obscurity. Often, it is in the darkest of times that it is easiest to see God.

Thick Cloud Pavlova

4 large egg whites
Pinch of salt
1 cup (200 g) sugar
1 tsp. white vinegar
½ tsp. vanilla
½ Tbsp. cornstarch
3 Tbsp. cocoa powder (optional—to darken the cloud)

Topping
1 cup (240 mL) whipping cream
1½ Tbsp. granulated white sugar
½ tsp. vanilla
1 cup (240 g) fresh fruit (optional—suggest kiwi slices,
   strawberries, raspberries, and/or blueberries)

Preheat oven to 250°F (130°C) and place rack in center of oven.

Line a baking sheet with parchment paper, and draw a 7-inch (18-cm) diameter circle on the paper.

Beat the egg whites with a pinch of salt with an electric mixer until peaks form. Continue beating, gradually adding sugar one tablespoon at a time, then add vinegar and vanilla, until a thick consistency is achieved. Test to make sure sugar is fully dissolved (if the mixture is grainy, then keep mixing). Lightly fold in cornstarch (and cocoa powder, if using).

Pile mixture into circular shape, making a hollow in the center for filling. Bake undisturbed for 1½ hours. Turn the oven off, leave the door slightly ajar, and let the meringue cool completely in the oven.

Just before serving, whip cream in electric mixer with the whisk attachment until soft peaks form. Fold in sugar and vanilla, and mound into center of meringue. Arrange fruit on top.

Serves 8–10.

ALTERNATIVES: Serve marshmallows, dark chocolate, chocolate covered marshmallows, and anything with whipped cream (which you can darken a bit with cinnamon or cocoa powder for effect).

QUESTIONS: Why did the people remain far away? Do you think you would have wanted to be close to the mountain? Why did God appear in a thick cloud? Why not in a pillar of fire? Aren't clouds a little gloomy?

Harvesting God's Kindness

You shall observe the festival of unleavened bread. For seven days you shall eat unleavened bread as I have commanded you, for the festival of the month of springtime, because you left Egypt then, and you shall not see my face empty-handed. And the harvest festival of your labor's first fruits that you sowed in the fields, and the ingathering festival at the end of the year, when you gather your work in from the field.

Exodus 23:15-16

Though most of the verses in chapter 23 have to do with civil law, a closer look at the text reveals that many of these laws relate to food. Not only are the Israelites commanded not to cook a kid in its mother's milk (the most obvious food reference), but they are commanded to let the land lie fallow every seven years and to make a pilgrimage to Jerusalem three times a year, each time for a different food-related reason.

The holidays are presented here as agricultural holidays. The Passover holiday is set in the springtime—the beginning of the growth season. The Festival of Weeks marks the harvesting of the first fruits, and the Tabernacle Festival falls at the end of harvest time.

Another element that stands out in chapter 23 is the number seven. Every seven years the land must lie fallow, the Passover holiday lasts for seven days, leading into the seven-week countdown to the Festival of Weeks, the first fruit offering given on the Festival of Weeks can only be brought from the seven species of the land of Israel, and the Tabernacle Holiday lasts for seven days. What is the relationship between the civil laws, the agricultural festivals and the number seven?

God created the world in seven days with the intention of having us continue to reinvent this seven-day-week model for all eternity. The number seven is the basic center of our day-to-day existence. The seasons, the holidays—everything exists within the realm of the seven-day week, and it is God who created the template. The same way that God asks us to emulate him by resting on the Sabbath, every seven years we are to emulate God by resting the land, thereby giving the poor an opportunity to take food (Exodus 23:11). Just as on the Sabbath we are supposed to acknowledge that God sustains the world by not working, when we let the land lie fallow we acknowledge that the land and all its produce belong to God and are at his mercy, not ours.

The three agricultural festivals emphasize and celebrate this concept. These festivals symbolize three ideas: freedom, the seasons, and prosperity. We celebrate Passover for seven days to usher in the spring and to remember that we owe our birth as a people to God. We count seven weeks leading up to the Festival of Weeks and then revel in the bounty of the seven species. We celebrate the harvest by moving out of our homes and into the fields on the Tabernacle Festival—acknowledging that we are utterly dependent on God's benevolence and even our permanent dwellings are temporary.

Seven-Species Harvest Chicken

2 onions, chopped

2 Tbsp. olive oil

1 tsp. cinnamon

1 tsp. ground ginger

2 chickens, cut into eighths

½ cup (65 g) flour

1 cup dried whole figs

1 cup (240 g) dried whole
dates

1 cup (240 mL) white wine

1 cup (240 mL)
pomegranate juice

1 cup (200 g) barley

2 cups (475 mL) chicken
stock

1 cup (230 g) almonds or
pecans (optional)

Salt and pepper, to taste

Sauté onions in olive oil in a large pot. Add cinnamon and ginger. Toss chicken in a bowl with flour, then add chicken to pot and brown on all sides. (This may need to be done in shifts, according to the size of your pot.) Return all chicken pieces to the pot and add remaining ingredients. Cook 45–60 minutes or until chicken has cooked through.

Serves 8–10.

ALTERNATIVES: Serve everything at your table in multiples of seven. Make sure to only invite seven guests! Serve seven layer cake, seven layer salad, or seven vegetable soup. Put seven types of fruit in your fruit salad, or serve all seven species: wheat, barley, grapes, figs, pomegranates, olives, dates.

QUESTIONS: Why are so many of our holidays connected to food? Why are they always connected to a specific time of year? What is the significance of the harvest? What is so special about the number seven? Is it central to our lives? Why?

A Dual Monarchy?

And they shall make an ark of acacia wood, two and a half cubits in length and one and a half cubits in width and a cubit and a half in height. And you shall cover it in pure gold, within and without, and you shall make upon it a golden crown all around.

Exodus 25:10-11

We encounter two crowns in two very unlikely places in chapter 25 of Exodus. One crown surrounds a golden ark, and the other, a golden table. Both the table and the ark are components of the tabernacle that traveled through the desert with the Israelites for forty years.

Commentators explain that the first crown is the symbol of the crown of the Bible. The holy ark houses the Ten Commandments, the essence and symbol of the Bible, and the Israelites are a nation only by virtue of the Bible.

The table's crown, on the other hand, according to commentators, is symbolic of the crown of kingship, for the table represents wealth and greatness. Since the day that God created the world, his blessings express themselves in the physical world through objects that humankind can relate to—in this case, a table.

This table and the twelve loaves of bread that sit on it are the origin of the blessing through which all of Israel will be satiated.

In essence these two crowns represent our spiritual and physical needs. The first crown surrounds the ark, representing the crown of the Bible—the raiment that we wear as a people and through which we gain our spiritual strength.

The crown surrounding the table represents both our kingship in the physical sense—the leaders who guide the Israelites throughout the years—and the source of all of our material blessing.

Golden Potato, Leek, and Salmon Crown

1 2.2 lb. (1 kg) pkg. frozen puff pastry dough
1 large leek, sliced thin
1 Tbsp. olive oil
1 Tbsp. fresh dill, chopped
Salt and pepper, to taste

4 potatoes, sliced very thin
½ lb. (240 g) smoked salmon
Juice of ½ lemon
1 egg, beaten

Preheat oven to 400°F (200°C). Grease a 9-inch (23 cm) round baking dish or pie plate.

Spread half of puff pastry dough into the bottom of a round baking dish or pie plate. Cut off a portion of the remaining dough into triangles, and arrange around the sides of the round dish so that one point of each triangle sticks up. Reserve the rest of the dough. Sauté leek in olive oil until limp, add salt and pepper to taste, then add fresh dill and cook 1–2 minutes more. Spread leek onto dough in baking dish. Sprinkle potato slices with salt and pepper and arrange on top of the leeks. Top with slices of smoked salmon and drizzle with lemon juice. Cover tart with remaining puff pastry dough, join at edges and cut 2–3 decorative slits into top of tart. Brush tart with beaten egg. Bake uncovered for 30–35 minutes or until puffy and golden.

Serves 8.

ALTERNATIVES: Cut crown shapes out of puff pastry dough, sprinkle with cinnamon and sugar, and bake until golden. Shape bread dough into a round crown shape. Spread a golden tablecloth on your table and make some homemade paper crowns for decoration.

QUESTIONS: Why do we encounter two crowns in chapter 25—one crown around an ark and another around a table? This seems very strange. What could be the significance? What furniture in your house should be crowned? Is there a reason to crown something other than a person? What does a crown represent?

Pure Light

And you shall command the children of Israel, and they shall bring to you
pure pressed olive oil for illumination, for the kindling of light, eternally.

Exodus 27:20

In chapters 25–26 the Israelites are asked to make
donations to the Tabernacle. Suggestions of appropriate
gifts are enumerated: gold, silver, copper, expensive
spices, precious jewels and more. In chapter 27, the
children of Israel are commanded to bring olive oil—a
commodity far less expensive than the items they
donated freely. They are also commanded not to bring
just any old olive oil, but rather the biblical version
of extra virgin. This special oil is to be used for the
lighting of an "eternal" menorah or candelabra, yet the
Tabernacle, by definition, was a temporary structure.
The verse begs interpretation.

The obligatory bringing of the olive oil and its use in
the kindling of the menorah are intended to impart to
us something far more valuable than its material worth,
explain the commentators. There are five expressions
in Hebrew that describe the type of olive oil needed
for kindling the menorah—"*shemen zayit zach katit
lama'or*" (pure olive oil, pressed, for lighting)—these,
say one commentator, represent the various character
traits of the Israelites.

Oil (*shemen*) rises to the top just as the Israelites
rise to every situation or challenge. The olive (*zayit*)
tree does not shed its leaves, symbolizing the eternity
of the children of Israel in both this world and the
world to come. Pure (*zach*) oil does not mix with
other substances, just as the children of Israel keep
themselves apart from the other nations.

Just as the olive must be pressed (*katit*) in order to extract the oil, so too the Israelites will occasionally experience hardships that will only serve to release the "oil" inside them and aid their return to God. "For lighting" (*lama'or*)—it is through this process of oil extraction that the Israelites become a light unto the nations.

The process of the extraction of this extra virgin olive oil and its use for lighting the physical menorah is merely practice for the spiritual work that the children of Israel need to do: to make the menorah "eternal" by extracting the light from their souls and illuminating the world with God's light. As it says in Isaiah 60:3, "Nations will walk by your light and kings by the brilliance of your shine."

Extra Virgin Olive Marinade

1 cup (240 g) black olives
1 cup (240 g) green olives
1 cup (240 mL) extra virgin olive oil
Juice and zest of 1 lemon
5 cloves garlic, thinly sliced
¼ cup (2 oz./60 g) fresh parsley or cilantro, chopped
1 tsp. oregano
Red pepper flakes, to taste

Combine all ingredients and let them sit overnight. It's best to use a self-sealing bag, but a container with a good solid seal of any kind will do. Shake up the bag or container once or twice during the marinating process. Serve the marinated olives with some fresh pita or a loaf of crusty bread.

Serves 4–6.

ALTERNATIVES:
Anything made with extra virgin olive oil or olives, "light" food items.

QUESTIONS: Why does the Bible specify that the olive oil must be "pure" and "pressed"? Why olive oil and not any other type of oil? What is special about oil? How was this menorah (or candelabra) eternal? What does the Bible mean by eternal?

All That Glitters . . .

And he took it from their hands, and he formed it with a chisel and he made it into a molten calf, and they said: "This is your god, O Israel, who brought you up from the land of Egypt!"
Exodus 32:4

When Moses does not come down from Mount Sinai on the day that the Israelites expect him, they begin to panic. They say to Aaron, "Come on! Make us gods that will go before us, because this man Moses, who brought us up from the land of Egypt, we don't know what has become of him" (Exodus 32:1). Aaron thinks fast and agrees to help the people build a golden calf. Secretly, says one commentator, he hoped that the process of collecting the gold, melting it down, engraving it, and shaping it into a calf would be enough of a stall tactic to keep the people occupied until Moses descended from the mountain with the Ten Commandments.

That Aaron should allow the people to construct an idol just as a way to pass the time is a bit troubling. But another commentator has a wiser take on this quandary. Aaron was afraid for his life, he explains, and the sin of murder is a far graver one than the sin of forging a graven image, which can be forgiven after proper repentance on the part of the sinner. Furthermore, Aaron never intended that the people would worship the golden calf. It is only after he fashions the idol that the people enthusiastically say, "This is your god, O Israel, who brought you up from the land of Egypt!" (Exodus 32:4). Aaron immediately builds an altar in front of the calf and responds to this call by correcting them and saying, "Tomorrow shall be a festival to the Lord" (32:5).

Aaron didn't think that the people would actually worship the idol; he had hoped that the idol would stand as a representation of God and that the people would worship God through the golden calf.

But things got out of hand.

The next morning, the people got up early to begin the festivities. They "offered up burnt offerings, and brought peace offerings, and the people sat down to eat and to drink, and they got up to make merry" (Exodus 32:6). When Moses finally makes his descent, with the tablets of the Ten Commandments in his hands, Joshua says to him, "There is a voice of battle in the camp!" (Exodus 32:17). The revelry had gotten out of control, and indeed when Moses sees the camp it is "the calf and the dances" (32:19) that cause him to fling the tablets from his hands.

Festive Golden Brisket

2.2 lb. (1 kg) brisket
2 Tbsp. oil
2 onions, chopped
½ cup (100 g) brown sugar
¼ tsp. salt
¼ tsp. pepper
4 cups (960 mL) boiling water
3–4 sweet potatoes, peeled and cut into chunks
6 carrots, peeled and cut into chunks
2 apples, peeled and sliced
3 potatoes, peeled and cut into chunks
½ cup (120 g) apricot or orange jam
¼ cup (60 mL) ketchup
1 Tbsp. cornstarch
1 Tbsp. mustard
1 11 oz. (312 g) can mandarin orange sections

Brown meat in oil in a large, wide pot or roasting pan.
Add onions, ½ cup brown sugar, salt, and pepper. Stir
in boiling water. Cover and cook for 2 hours. Add sweet
potatoes, carrots, apples, and potatoes. In a separate
bowl, mix together remaining brown sugar, apricot or
orange jam, ketchup, cornstarch, and mustard. Mix
well. Add entire can of mandarin orange sections,
including liquid. Pour half of the sauce over the meat
and cook for 1 more hour. Pour remaining sauce over
meat and cook until meat is tender. Let meat cool, slice
thin, and serve garnished with vegetables and sauce.

Serves 6–8.

ALTERNATIVES: Serving
any kind of roast or beef,
even meatloaf will do to
represent the calf.
Set your table with a
golden tablecloth or
table runner, decorate the
table with gold confetti
or golden napkin rings—
anything glittery or sparkly
with which to decorate
your table—or your
meatloaf!

QUESTIONS: Why do you
think that Aaron agreed to
help make the golden calf?
Is he as much to blame as
the people were? It seems
so out of character for
Aaron to agree to this! What
do you think happened?
Have you ever been in a
situation when you have
done something against
your better judgment?
What happened?

A Tapestry of Talent

And Moses said to the Israelites: "See, that God has called upon the name Bezalel son of Uri, son of Hur, of the tribe of Judah. And he has filled him with the spirit of God, with wisdom, with insight, and with knowledge, and with all manner of craftsmanship; to create master weaving, to work with gold, silver, and copper."

Exodus 35:30-32

This chapter of the Bible details the attributes and skills of Bezalel and Oholiav, the two master craftsmen responsible for the architecture, construction, and art direction necessary to build the Tabernacle. It is interesting to note that as the first artist mentioned in the Bible, Bezalel is described as having wisdom, insight, knowledge and the spirit of God in addition to talent. Not only that, but as one commentator explains, Bezalel was able to hear and learn from others. He was blessed with deep understanding from within, divine inspiration, and the ability to design, to carve, and to match stones and settings perfectly. In essence he is the prototype for the perfect artist.

Why did the Bible need to tell us all of this? Isn't it obvious that God would appoint someone talented to build the Tabernacle? Another commentator states that what was unique about Bezalel was that even though the only work the Israelites knew how to do as slaves in Egypt was to build with bricks and mortar, Bezalel knew how to work with gold and silver, gemstones, wood and weaving cloth. He was an artist who, despite adversity, was able to let his gifts shine.

It is said that not only was Bezalel talented, but he literally had God-given gifts—he was able to weave the letters that God used during creation to divine precisely what God wanted him to create. More important than that, God "put it into Bezalel's heart to teach" (Exodus 35:34). The mark of a great artist is not only his work, but his ability and desire to pass on his skills and imbue others with his passion.

Woven Tapestry Bread

2 Tbsp. dry yeast
1¾ cups (414 mL)
    warm water
Pinch of sugar
5 cups (625 g) flour
2 tsp. salt
2 Tbsp. cocoa powder

4 Tbsp. butter or
    margarine, melted
2 Tbsp. molasses
2 Tbsp. honey
1 egg
Sesame and poppy seeds
    (optional)

Preheat oven to 350°F (180°C).

In two separate bowls place 1 Tbsp. yeast and ½ cup warm water with a pinch of sugar. Allow yeast to froth—about 5 minutes. Add 2½ cups flour and 1 tsp. salt to each bowl.

Into one of the bowls, add cocoa powder, ½ cup warm water, 2 Tbsp. butter, and 2 Tbsp. molasses. Mix together until a soft dough forms. Place dough into an oiled bowl. Cover and allow to rise in a warm place for 1 hour or until doubled in bulk.

Into the other bowl, add ¼ cup warm water, 2 Tbsp. butter, and 2 Tbsp. honey. Mix together until a soft dough forms. Add more flour as needed until dough is soft, yet smooth and elastic, and not too sticky. Place dough into an oiled bowl. Cover and allow to rise in a warm place for 1 hour or until doubled in bulk.

Punch down and knead each ball of dough. Form each ball of dough into five 6-inch snakes or rolled strips. Weave dark strips through white strips to form a large square.

Cover dough and let rise until doubled in size—about 45 minutes. Lightly beat egg and brush over top of bread. Sprinkle alternating colors with sesame and poppy seeds (sesame seeds on the dark dough and poppy seeds on the light dough). Bake 20–25 minutes or until bread is nicely browned.

Serves 6–8.

ALTERNATIVES: Serve Triscuit crackers or Rice/Corn Chex, or make Crispix Mix—any kind of cracker or cereal that has a woven form to it will do. Cut basic sugar cookies (from a mix or ready made from a tube) into letter shapes and have your guests and/or children "weave" with them, or decorate the cookies into works of art with candy "gemstones" (sugar crystals, sprinkles and silver candy balls). Different color strands of cooked fettuccini, Twizzlers, or fruit roll-up strips can also be woven.

QUESTIONS: Why does the Bible need to tell us that Bezalel was talented? Isn't obvious that God would choose someone talented to build the tabernacle (*mishkan*)? And anyway, then it tells us that God gave him wisdom, insight, knowledge and talent, so was he really talented? Are all gifts God-given?

A Heavenly Burden

And they brought the Tabernacle to Moses, the tent and all its utensils:
its hooks, its planks, its bars, its pillars, and its sockets.
Exodus 39:33

Many of the chapters of the book of Exodus discuss the building of the Tabernacle. But here in chapter 39, we see the culmination of the building process. However, the above verse is strange, why did the people need to bring the Tabernacle to Moses? Why couldn't they just assemble it themselves when all the work was done and all its components completed? Commentators suggest that since Moses had not done any physical work on the Tabernacle himself, God left the last job for him.

They commentators also suggest that nobody was able to set up the Tabernacle because of the weight of the boards. But this is puzzling. How can it be that the people were able to transport the boards to Moses, but they could not assemble them? Also, why couldn't the men work together to assemble the Tabernacle? Certainly ten men working together would be stronger than Moses working alone.

The answer given is that the difficulty in raising the Tabernacle had nothing to do with its physical weight, but rather its spiritual weight. The Tabernacle was a microcosm of the world, a physical representation of the world that contained the Holy Ark, which was why only God (through Moses) could assemble it.

After the construction of the golden calf, the Israelites donated freely and actively involved themselves in the construction of the Tabernacle. It therefore held a part of each and every person in it. The process of building the Tabernacle was a form of

spiritual rehabilitation, and so it was weighed down with the physical and spiritual contributions of every one of the people.

* The gingerbread tabernacle you see pictured here would not have been possible without the help of Dina Grossman.

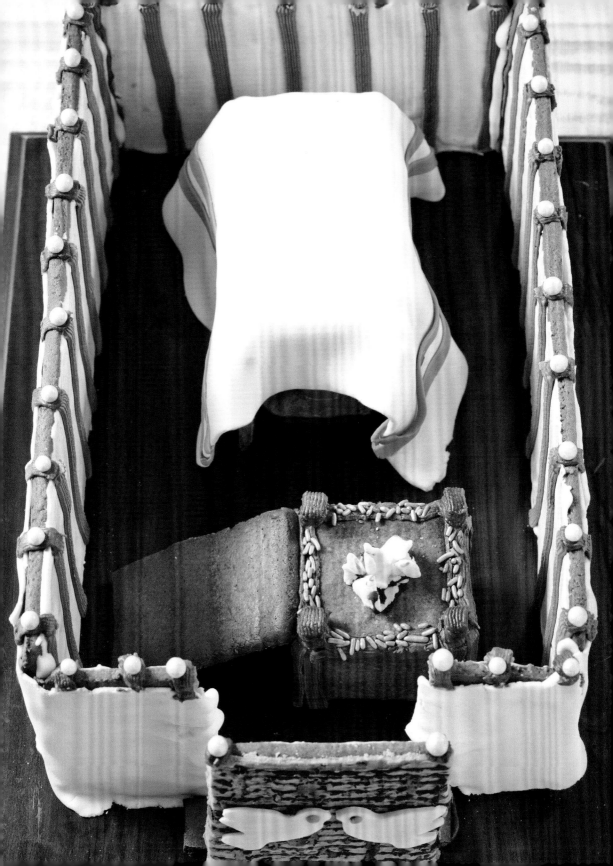

A Gingerbread Tabernacle

Dough

1 cup (226 g) butter or margarine

1 cup (200 g) sugar

1 cup (240 mL) molasses or corn syrup

2 eggs

1 tsp. baking soda

1 tsp. salt

½ tsp. nutmeg

3 tsp. ginger

2 tsp. cinnamon

½ tsp. ground cloves

5 cups (675 g) flour

Royal Icing

2 egg whites

2–3 cups (½ kg) powdered sugar

Prepared white fondant

Prepared fondant in red, yellow, blue, and purple

Gold sprinkles, white/silver candy balls, edible gold glitter/powder

Preheat oven to 350°F (180°C).

Dough: Melt butter, add sugar and molasses. Mix together, then add eggs. Stir in baking soda and spices, mix, and then add flour slowly until you have a stiff dough.

Roll out to about ¼ inch (1 cm) thick and cut out shapes. Make sure each same type of shape is the same size.

> 2 large long rectangles: approx. 4 x 12 inches (10 x 30 cm)
>
> 2 large short rectangles: approx. 4 x 8 inches (10 x 20 cm)
>
> 5 small squares: approx. 3 x 3 inches (7.5 x 7.5 cm)
>
> 4 small rectangles: approx. 3 x 5 inches (7.5 x 12.5 cm)

Bake for 10–13 minutes on a cookie sheet. Remove when cold.

Icing: Whip egg whites into stiff peaks, then add powdered sugar 1/4 cup at a time.

Optional: Small silver candy balls for decoration. Brown food coloring or cocoa powder to turn icing brown. Bird-shaped cutters.

To assemble:

Tabernacle: Make a large open-top rectangle, using the two large long rectangles as the sides and two of the large short rectangles as the front and back, breaking the front rectangle into three pieces—two for the sides of the entrance and one for the center. The front center panel can be frosted purple and red, and you can make it look woven or ice on some birds. This can also be done with fondant (as pictured). Roll out a very long piece of white fondant which you will then wrap around the entire outer perimeter of the tabernacle. Pipe with brown frosting to make pillars and decorate the tops of these pillars with silver candy balls.

Ark: Join three small rectangles (two for the sides and one on top). Place the ark in the back of the Tabernacle. Roll out white fondant, and "tent" it on top of the ark. You can also roll out two strips of blue fondant for decoration. You can mold a yellow fondant candelabra (or cut one out with a menorah cookie cutter) and paint it with edible gold glitter. Place this inside the ark.

Altar: Join five small squares to form a box and attach one small rectangle as a ramp. Place the altar in the larger area of the Tabernacle. Pipe with brown frosting and decorate with golden sprinkles. You can mold yellow and red fondant into a little "fire" with "flames."

Serves 10–12.

ALTERNATIVES: Use Petit-Buerre cookies or graham crackers to have children and adults at your table assemble their own mini versions of the tabernacle (*mishkan*) using ready made frosting as the "glue". This can also be done after dinner with a deck of cards or dominoes (minus the frosting!).

QUESTIONS: Why was the tabernacle brought to Moses? Wasn't he involved all along? Did it need his approval? Didn't he approve everything already? What now was Moses's task?

Leviticus

Spiritually Salty

And you shall season every meal-offering with salt, do not discontinue the salt of the covenant of God from your meal offering–on all your sacrifices you shall offer salt.

Leviticus 2:13

Now that the Tabernacle has been dedicated, the real work begins. The beginning of Leviticus outlines the basic directives for offering sacrifices. Every sacrifice is different, according to the intention of the sacrifice, the type of animal offered, and the financial status of the person making the sacrifice, but there is one thing that all sacrifices have in common: salt.

One commentator's explanation of this oddity is even more strange than the thing itself. He does not attempt to explain that salt enhances the taste of food, or that salt acts as a preservative—explanations that make logical sense. The commentator instead states that when God separated the upper waters from the lower waters (Genesis 1:6–8), the lower waters complained (believing that they would be "demoted"). In response, God made a covenant with the lower waters that their salt would be offered on the altar and that their waters would be offered as a libation during the Tabernacle holiday.

A different commentator also offers a somewhat esoteric explanation. According to him, a sacrifice, in order to completely elevate humankind and the world, needs to include an element from all aspects of creation: inanimate, vegetable, animal and human. Salt represents the inanimate world, grain—the vegetable; the animal being sacrificed—the animal world; and the human—who offers up the sacrifice itself.

Another commentator's approach is a bit more down to earth. According to him, salt has the power to be constructive or destructive. Salt can prevent plants from growing, but it can also preserve food. The inclusion of salt as a part of every sacrifice teaches us that sacrifices have the potential to preserve us or to destroy us. In order for them to preserve our spirit, they must be offered with the right spiritual intentions.

Herb-Roasted Beef in a Salt Crust

¼ cup (60 mL) olive oil
1 onion, minced fine
1 tsp. garlic powder (or 2–3 cloves fresh garlic, crushed)
1 tsp. dried (or 1 Tbsp. fresh) basil
1 tsp. dried (or 1 Tbsp. fresh) marjoram
1 tsp. dried (or 1 Tbsp. fresh) thyme
1 tsp. dried (or 1 Tbsp. fresh) rosemary
½ tsp. pepper
4–5 lb. (2.5 kg) shoulder roast
3 lb. (1.4 kg) box coarse (kosher) salt
1¼ cups (300 mL) water

Combine oil, onion, garlic, basil, marjoram, thyme, rosemary, and pepper in heavy plastic bag. Add roast and shake it up a bit. Marinate in refrigerator at least two hours or (preferably) overnight.

Preheat oven to 425°F (220°C).

Line a large roasting pan with aluminum foil. Combine salt and water to form a thick paste. Place 1 cup of paste on bottom of pan and press down. Place roast on salt layer and spread the remaining salt paste to cover and seal the meat completely.

Place roast in oven and roast for 2 hours (more if you like your meat well done). Remove from oven and let sit 10–15 minutes. Tap salt crust until it cracks (you may need a hammer), remove crust and brush off all salt crystals. Carve and serve. Contrary to what you might think, the salt does not make for salty meat—it acts to seal in the flavors and the juice.

ALTERNATIVES: Encrust your steak, burger, or meatloaf with a salty rub (most steak spices are pretty salty on their own), or serve a bowl of salt at the table for dipping, just don't forget to eat your meat with the right intentions!

QUESTIONS: Why do nearly all sacrifices include salt? What is it about salt that makes it spiritual or necessary? Is it a preservative? Does it enhance the taste of the meat? Why would God desire salt?

Humility and Care

And Moses took the anointing oil and he anointed the Sanctuary and everything in it and he made them holy … And he poured some of the anointing oil upon Aaron's head, and he anointed him, to sanctify him.

Leviticus 8:10-12

One commentator explains that Moses first poured the oil on Aaron's head, then between his eyelids, then he spread the oil with his finger from one eyelid to the other. Why do we need a detailed explanation about how the oil was poured and smeared on Aaron's face?

The Babylonian Talmud relates an interesting anecdote. When Moses anointed Aaron as the first high priest, a bit of oil dripped down onto Aaron's beard. Moses worried that he might have wasted even that little bit of the sanctified oil. A heavenly voice then called out and said, "It is like the dew of the Hermon, that falls upon the mountains of Zion."

Just as the law of improper use of holy objects does not apply to the dew of Hermon, so too the law is not applicable to the oil on Aaron's beard. Nevertheless, Aaron was still anxious. He said, maybe Moses did not sin, but perhaps I have wasted the oil. Another heavenly voice called out, "How good and how pleasant it is for brothers to sit together, as the good oil upon the head, which falls down upon the beard of Aaron and falls down upon his clothes."

This commentator was perhaps trying to explain how it may have come to be that the oil dripped on to Aaron's beard—in the process of the pouring and then smearing from eyelid to eyelid. But apparently this was also not just any oil. The oil that was used to anoint Aaron and the Tabernacle was a special mixture of oils, spices, and perfumes that was made by Moses in Exodus, chapter 30. That oil was described as "an anointing oil sacred to me throughout the generations" (Exodus 30:31).

This original batch of oil used to anoint Aaron, the Tabernacle, and every king was intended to someday anoint the Messiah, and this oil will hopefully carry together with it the (moral) lessons of Moses and Aaron.

Moses was once scheduled to receive the priesthood, but he loses the privilege in Exodus 4:14, when he argues with God and does not want to be the one to take the people out of Egypt. Yet he is the one who anoints Aaron and his sons. This must have been a difficult task, knowing full well that he could have been anointing his own sons were it not for his own folly. However, Moses and Aaron were so humble that even at a moment that could have been fraught with jealousy and ill will, the brothers' only concern was whether they wasted a few drops of the precious oil. If only all our disputes would be so small.

Anointed Vegetables

3 or 4 red bell peppers, roasted and peeled, or 1 large jar
    roasted red peppers
12 mushrooms, sliced
15 cherry tomatoes, halved
1 cup (240 g) pitted olives, green or black
¼ cup (60 g) fresh basil, chopped
2 heads of garlic, crushed
2 Tbsp. balsamic vinegar
1 cup (240 g) artichoke hearts or bottoms
Salt and pepper, to taste
6 Tbsp. olive oil

Combine peppers, mushrooms, tomatoes, olives, basil, garlic, and balsamic vinegar. Add artichoke hearts or bottoms (undrained). Add salt and pepper to taste, and then anoint the mixture with olive oil. Mix all ingredients together and marinate at least 1 hour before serving. For effect you can leave out 1 Tbsp. of olive oil and anoint the salad with the oil at your table. It's a great way to spark conversation.

Serves 4–6.

ALTERNATIVES: If you don't have time to make a marinade or a recipe using a marinade—buy a jar of something marinated. Anoint something you serve with olive oil at the table—put olive oil on olives, on hummus, on your salad, put out a bowl of olive oil and balsamic vinegar for dipping your bread into.

QUESTIONS: Why did Moses pour oil on Aaron's head? Why is oil sacred? Why is it used to sanctify objects and people?

Out for a Swim

And this you shall eat, from all that is in the water: Anything that has fins and scales in the water, in the seas and the streams, those you may eat. And anything that does not have fins and scales in the water, in the seas and the stream, of all that swarm the waters, and from all the living things that are in the water, they are an abomination for you.

Leviticus 11:9-10

Verses 9–10 of Leviticus, chapter 11, describe the types of fish that are permitted. The only requirement, however, is that fish must have both fins and scales. Why does it take four verses to explain this simple dictum?

Many commentators ask the same question. One highlights the fact that we are told that we may eat creatures that have fins and scales "that are in the water." Without the verses that come after this one, we might think that a creature that lives in the water is only permitted to if it has fins and scales both in and out of the water. The other verses come to explain that "any creature that does not have fins and scales in the water is an abomination for you," but if the fish had fins and scales in the water, and it sheds them upon emerging from the water, it is still permitted.

These verses are often used as proof of the Bible's brilliance—not only are all fish that have fins and scales permitted, but there are no fish in existence that have only scales and no fins. However, this is not the case.

There are varieties of fish that have scales but no fins, often immature fish do not yet have scales, and some fish lose their scales when they emerge from the water.

We have to dig a little deeper.

Another commentator states that every person needs both fins and scales and that is what God is trying to tell us here. Fins are essential in order for a person to move forward in his studies, his wisdom and his intellect. The scales are critical because they symbolize fear of heaven; they are the armor that protects each person from his enemies and his evil inclination.

A person with fins and no scales is not a permitted fish. He might revel in intellectual pursuits but without the fear of heaven his belief is corrupt. On the other hand, we are led to believe that all fish with scales have fins; meaning that if a person fears God then he will succeed in life.

A sardine is a good example of a fish that loses its scales but is still considered a permitted fish.

Mediterranean Sardine Shells

1 lb. (454 g) bag or box pasta, shells or penne
½ cup (120 g) black olives, pitted and chopped
1 4.375 oz. (125 g) can sardines packed in oil, drained
2 cloves garlic, crushed
1 cup (240 g) marinated artichoke hearts or bottoms
½ cup (120 g) sun-dried tomatoes in olive oil
Crushed red pepper flakes, to taste
3 Tbsp. olive oil (or as needed)
Salt and pepper, to taste
Dash of balsamic vinegar
¼ cup (60 g) parsley, chopped

Cook and drain pasta and place in a bowl. In a separate bowl, combine rest of ingredients. The sardines will break apart while you mix. Toss pasta with sauce and serve.

Serves 4–6.

ALTERNATIVES: Cook an entire fish, head, scales, fins, and all (gutted of course), and use that as the conversation piece at your table. Whole sardines, sardine spread, or pâté could work too, and gummy fish if fish are not your thing at all . . .

QUESTIONS: Why must fish have fins and scales? What is it about fins and scales? Why those distinguishing characteristics? What do they represent?

Words of Wisdom

If a man has a raised area, a scab, or a spot on the skin of his flesh, and it forms a lesion of leprosy on his skin, he shall be brought to Aaron the High Priest, or to one of his Priestly Sons.

Leviticus 13:2

Commentators explain that leprosy only comes as a punishment for the sin of evil speech. Yet there is certainly no other affliction or punishment in the Bible that is described in such tedious and graphic detail. Why dedicate an entire chapter to a skin condition? Most commentators explain that leprosy was a spiritual disease.

Someone who has leprosy is called a *metzora*, and commentators explain that the word is an acronym for the Hebrew words *motzi shem ra*—one who tarnishes the reputation of another. The Jerusalem Talmud states that there are three sins that a person is punished for in this world and in the next world—immorality, idolatry, and murder. But speaking badly about others is equal to all three because evil speech destroys a person emotionally, spiritually, and physically.

Thus the leper is different from any other impure individual, commentators explain. When someone is ritually impure they are not banished from the camp, but a leper must be separated out because his evil speech caused rifts between husbands and wives, family members, friends, and neighbors.

The reason that the leper must be brought to the High Priest to obtain a diagnosis is because since the leper sinned with words, he can only be purified through the pronouncements of the High Priest. Only once his

leprosy (and the sin that caused it) is discovered and acknowledged can he begin the process of spiritual and physical rehabilitation.

Cat's Got Your Tongue Cookies

½ cup (113 g) butter or margarine
½ cup (65 g) powdered sugar
2 egg whites
¼ tsp. salt
1 tsp. vanilla or almond extract
1 tsp. lemon zest (optional)
¾ cup (90 g) flour
1 cup (240 g) chocolate chips
1 Tbsp. corn syrup
½ cup (120 g) chopped nuts, sprinkles, or coconut
    (optional)

Preheat oven to 400 F° (200° C).

Cream butter and sugar together. Add egg whites gradually, beating well after each addition. Add salt and vanilla or almond extract, and lemon zest if using. Mix well, then add flour gradually. Place batter in a cake-decorating piping bag (or a ziplock bag with a hole cut out of one of the bottom corners) and form the dough into tongue-like shapes on a greased cookie sheet. Bake for 10 minutes or until golden brown.

Melt chocolate together with corn syrup. When cookies are cool, you can dip half of each cookie into the chocolate and then into the nuts, sprinkles, or coconut.

Makes 2–3 dozen cookies.

ALTERNATIVES: Make "spotted" or "tongue" cookies, or anything wrapped up in puff pastry dough, in a tortilla-type wrap, or even sushi which is wrapped in seaweed! (Lepers often wrapped themselves with many bandages.) See how long everyone at your table can go without speaking about someone else.

QUESTIONS: Why does the Bible devote so much attention to describing a skin condition in such vivid detail? What is it about leprosy that makes it worthy of such attention? What did leprosy punish?

The Healing Hyssop

As the priest commands, he shall take for the person that needs to be cleansed: two live, pure birds, a cedar stick, a strip of crimson wool, and hyssop.

Leviticus 14:4

Immediately after the celebrations that marked the dedication of the Tabernacle, and the detailing of all permitted animals, birds, and fish, the narrative of the Bible moves into a very detailed description of leprosy. Unlike any illness we know of today, this paranormal disease afflicted the skin, the home, and the personal belongings of someone who sinned by speaking in a derogatory manner.

Even stranger, the prescribed cure includes "two live clean birds, a cedar stick, a strip of crimson wool, and hyssop."

What does this all mean? How are we supposed to find meaning in the detailed, sometimes graphic, descriptions of the lesions of a disease that no longer afflicts us, and even more so, in its strange cure?

One commentator (14:4) gives his take on the ingredients of the potion. Birds are required because the disease is a punishment for derogatory chattering and birds chirp constantly. The cedar stick, crimson wool, and hyssop all symbolize the afflicted's haughtiness.

Another commentator explains how: The cedar stick teaches the person with leprosy that because he exhibited arrogance, exalting himself like a cedar tree, he should now be humbled like the hyssop which grows low to the ground and like the worm that gives crimson dye.

It is said that disparaging others often comes about because of vanity. If you feel a need to denigrate another person, it reflects badly on you and indicates a lack of humility. Self-aggrandizement at the expense of another person is on a very low moral level. In order to correct the sin of evil speech, it is not enough to apologize. The sinner must experience this uncomfortable and embarrassing disease and bizarre purification ritual in order to learn the lesson that ego-inflation through the ridiculing of others is not a biblical value.

The hyssop is generally recognized as the za'atar herb—a form of marjoram/oregano native to the Middle East. It is a very important plant in the Bible, as it is used in the red heifer purification process for those who have had contact with a dead body, and was used by the Israelites in Egypt to mark their doorposts with blood so that God would "pass over" their homes during the plague of the slaying of the firstborn.

Grape Leaves Stuffed with Za'atar, Goat Cheese, and Sun-Dried Tomato

1 16 oz. (454 g) jar grape leaves in brine
1 7 oz. (200 g) jar sun-dried tomato spread
1 log goat cheese (6.5 oz. or 180 g)
Za'atar spice mix (if your local grocery store doesn't carry
    it, plain oregano will work)
Olive oil
Lemon juice

Remove grape leaves from jar and rinse well to remove brine. Spread out onto paper towels to remove moisture. Spread a small amount of sun-dried tomato spread on the stem end of the grape leaf. Cut a small slice of goat cheese from the log and place it in the middle of the grape leaf. Sprinkle with za'atar and drizzle with a little bit of olive oil. Roll up grape leaf around the goat cheese, tucking in the ends as you go. Arrange stuffed grape leaves on a platter and drizzle with olive oil and lemon juice before serving.

Makes 20–24 stuffed grape leaves.

ALTERNATIVES: Sprinkle pizza, pita, or focaccia with za'atar, and top with goat cheese and sun-dried tomatoes. Make a salad with goat cheese, sun-dried tomatoes, and za'atar. Rub chicken with za'atar and top with sun-dried tomatoes, then grill on a cedar plank.

QUESTIONS: Why do you think that the sin of speaking badly about someone else is so dire? Why is the punishment and cure so severe? Do you ever feel bad after you've said something negative about someone else? Why do you think that is?

Cliff Hanger

*And Aaron placed lots on the two goats: one lot "For the Lord," and the other lot, "For Azazel."
And Aaron shall sacrifice the goat on which the lot "For the Lord" comes up, and offer it as a sin
offering. And the goat on which the lot "For Azazel" comes up, shall stand alive before God, as
atonement for him, to send it to Azazel, to the desert.*

Leviticus 16:8-10

The question that these verses raise is, what in the world is Azazel? One commentator explains that the goat that went to Azazel was taken into the wilderness and cast off the cliffs, and based on the Babylonian Talmud, he parses Azazel as *azuz* (strong) and *el* (hard), relating to the sharp rocks at the bottom of the cliff. Another commentator sees the entire story as an allegory that warns the Israelites that the only place that sin leads to is a wasteland.

But why must this goat be sent off to the desert or cast off a cliff to atone for the sins of the people? Why doesn't a sacrifice suffice? Even stranger, commentators suggest that Azazel is not a place, but the angel Samael, "the dark prince"—an angel who rules over darkness and destruction.

How can it be that on the holiest day of the year, we offer a sacrifice to a dark angel?

One commentator offers an explanation that reconciles these opinions. He sees the goats as representing the Israelites's various states. When they follow God and refrain from sin they are like holy sacrifices to God. But when they sin and disobey God they are sent away from God's presence into the

wilderness. The people have two options: to serve God in piety and holiness, or to serve themselves; as one commentator puts it, Azazel represents a form of demon-worship—the barbarity and wildness that is part of human nature.

Acorn Squash Stuffed with Wild Rice and Goat Cheese

1 large acorn or butternut squash
½ cup (100 g) wild rice
½ cup (100 g) white rice
2 cups (475 mL) water
1 Tbsp. chicken soup powder
2 Tbsp. oil
1 onion, diced
2 cloves garlic, crushed
2 carrots, chopped
3 celery stalks, chopped
1 cup (230 g) mushrooms, chopped
2 Tbsp. (30 g) fresh parsley, chopped
1 tsp. dried thyme
¾ cup (180 g) goat cheese, crumbled, grated, or cubed

Preheat oven to 350°F (180°C).

Cut acorn squash in half and scoop out pits. Bake, cut side down, on foil-lined baking sheets for 30 minutes or until almost tender.

Bring wild rice, 1 cup water and chicken soup powder to a boil and cook until rice grains pop open. Drain and put aside. Cook white rice with remaining cup of water. Combine with wild rice.

Scoop out about half of the squash from each side of the cooked squash halves. Dice and sauté in oil with onion, garlic, carrots, and celery for about 5 minutes. Add mushrooms and cook 2–3 minutes more. Add parsley and thyme. Mix together with ½ cup goat cheese, combine with rice and restuff the squash halves. Top with remaining ¼ cup goat cheese. Bake for 10–15 minutes.

Serves 6–8.

ALTERNATIVES: Serve goat's cheese, goat's milk, or anything made with goat products; you can also serve anything "wild" like wild rice, wild honey, free-range chicken or beef, wild strawberries, wild mushrooms; or place wildflowers at your table to represent the wilderness of Azazel.

QUESTIONS: What is Azazel? Why must a goat be cast off into Azazel? Why does a sacrifice not suffice?

The Corner Store

And when you reap the harvest of your land, do not completely reap one corner of your
field, and the fallen stalks of your harvest do not gather. And your vineyard,
do not glean, nor gather the fallen grapes of your vineyard; leave them for the poor
and for the stranger: I am the Lord your God.

Leviticus 19:9-10

Amidst all the prohibitions that appear in Leviticus, in
this chapter we are commanded to be charitable in a
strange way. We are told to leave the remnants of our
fields for the poor. If God is taking the opportunity here
to command us to be charitable to the unfortunate—
why aren't we told to reap the harvest and then donate
a portion of the produce to the poor? Additionally, giving
to the poor is a logical thing to do. So why does God feel
the need to command us to do so by saying, "I am the
Lord your God"?

One commentator suggests that God wants to make
sure that the needy get what is rightfully theirs and
that we should know that God is a judge who exacts
punishment. Another commentator explains the same
words to mean that just as God exhibits the attributes
of kindness, we need to emulate the same traits. As
it says, "You shall be holy because I, your God, am
Holy," (Leviticus 19:2) and part of being holy is being
charitable. Still, why does God need to give us such
specific instructions?

The command to leave a corner of your field for the
poor along with the remnants of the field and the lone
grapes is there to teach the giver something. When you

leave a portion of your field for the poor, you do not know whom will come and gather your crop. You do not know who you are giving to, and there will be no thank-you note. You gain no personal benefit from this donation. It is the ultimate form of charity. God works in the same way—he does not expect any returns on his charity to us.

Other commentators suggest that another important aspect of this charitable act is allowing the poor to help themselves. You are not giving the poor person a prescribed amount—you are allowing him to come and harvest for himself. God's commandment here preserves the poor man's dignity.

Vineyard Chicken

6 skinless, boneless chicken breasts (about 2 lb. or 1 kg)

½ tsp. salt

½ tsp. dried basil

¼ tsp. dried tarragon

¼ tsp. paprika

Pepper to taste

2 Tbsp. flour

1 Tbsp. olive oil

2 cloves garlic, crushed

½ cup (120 g) mushrooms, sliced thin

½ cup (120 mL) chicken broth

½ cup (120 mL) dry white wine

½ cup (120 mL) soy milk or cream

1 tsp. lemon juice

2 cups (480 g) seedless grapes, halved

1 Tbsp. fresh parsley, chopped

Grape clusters for decoration

Cut each chicken breast in half, lengthwise, or flatten with a meat mallet. Blend together salt, basil, tarragon, paprika, pepper, and flour. Heat olive oil in a frying pan. Dip chicken pieces in flour mixture and brown in pan. Remove chicken from pan and set aside. Add garlic and mushrooms to pan and let cook 1–2 minutes on low flame. Add leftover flour, chicken broth, white wine, soy milk or cream, and lemon juice. Mix well and bring to a simmer. Cook 5 minutes until sauce has thickened. Return chicken to the pan and let cook another 5 minutes. Add grapes and parsley, and let cook 2–3 more minutes. Serve garnished with small grape clusters.

Serves 6–8.

ALTERNATIVES: Serve an abundance of grapes—take all the grapes off of their stems except for one cluster. Serve raisins or grapes on a square plate and leave one corner empty. You can really do this for effect with everything you serve—leave one corner of the brownie tray "unharvested," don't eat the last slice of meatloaf, etc.

QUESTIONS: Why is giving "leftovers" to the poor a charitable deed? Why are we not commanded to give the best of our crops and food to the poor? And isn't it obvious that we must be charitable to those less fortunate than us? Why must God tell us this? And why isn't it enough to just tell us to be charitable and not to tell us exactly how to do it?

Sanctifying the Holidays

Speak to the children of Israel and say to them: The holidays of God, that you shall designate as holy occasions–these are my holy days. For six days, you may perform work, and on the seventh day, it is a complete rest day, a holy occasion; you shall not perform any work. It is a Sabbath to the Lord in all your dwelling places. These are the holidays of God, which you shall designate in their appointed time.

Leviticus 23:2-4

Leviticus 23 is known as the portion of the festivals. The holidays of Passover, the Festival of Weeks, "a memorial of blowing trumpets," the Day of Atonement, and the Tabernacle Festival are all listed together. But already in the first few verses of the chapter, we have a question. Verse 2 says, "The Lord's appointed holy days that you shall designate as holy occasions—these are my appointed holy days," and what we expect to follow is a list of holidays. Instead, verse 3 tells us about the Sabbath. Verse 4 then reiterates, "These are the Lord's appointed holy occasions, which you shall designate in their appointed time." Only then does the list of holidays begin.

What is going on here? Why is the Sabbath listed, and why do the verses repeat themselves? One commentator's take is that the Sabbath is mentioned here to teach us that the desecration of a festival is equal to the desecration of the Sabbath, and vice versa—whoever fulfills all the obligations of the festivals is considered as if he fulfilled the obligations of the Sabbath.

Another commentator focuses his question on the fact that the word *moadim*, a Hebrew word that has the connotation of time, is mentioned more than once. Why doesn't God just say simply, "these are the festivals (*hagim*) of the year?" He explains that even though these are God's holidays, like the verse says, it is only when we designate and proclaim them as holy days and designate the days on which they will be celebrated, that they become holy and become God's festivals.

In verse 2 we are told that we designate holidays as holy occasions, and what follows is the Sabbath; however verse 4 tells us to designate the rest of the holidays "in their appointed time." The Sabbath is a day whose holiness we are responsible for, but we do not determine the Sabbath's appointed time. On the holidays, however, we are given the opportunity to designate both their holiness and their appointed time. We are vital partners in the sanctification of these festivals.

Festival Salad with Honey Balsamic Vinaigrette

The following salad has elements of all the holidays listed in this chapter of the Bible: apples and honey for Rosh Hashana, cheese for the Festival of Weeks, goat cheese for the goat that is sacrificed on the Day of Atonement to atone for our sins, dates and lemon juice to represent the palm frond and citron associated with the Tabernacle Festival, and walnuts—commonly associated with Passover.

3 cups (600 g) baby greens
2 apples, sliced thin
1 log of goat cheese (6.5 oz./180 g), sliced into rounds

1 cup (240 g) cherry tomatoes, halved
1 cup (240 g) pitted dates, quartered
1 cup (240 g) walnut pieces, toasted

Honey Balsamic Vinaigrette

½ cup (120 mL) balsamic vinegar
1 Tbsp. honey
1 tsp. lemon juice

1 tsp. Dijon mustard
2 Tbsp. olive oil
Salt and pepper, to taste

Arrange salad ingredients on a large serving platter or on individual plates. First layer the baby greens, then the apple slices and goat cheese rounds, followed by the cherry tomatoes, dates, and walnuts.

Mix all vinaigrette ingredients together and shake vigorously. Drizzle over salad and serve.

Serves 6–8.

ALTERNATIVES: Serve items associated with each of the holidays mentioned above, apples dipped in honey, dairy products, an empty plate perhaps to symbolize the day of atonement, matzah for Passover, and a harvest food for the Tabernacle Festival. Alternatively you can serve food items that represent the weekend or the Sabbath to you—your favorite foods.

QUESTIONS: Though this chapter of the Bible starts out telling us about the holidays, the verses then go on to discuss the Sabbath—why would this be? What makes a holiday a special time? What makes the weekend or Sabbath a special time? What sanctifies a day and makes it holy?

Let Freedom Ring

And you shall count for yourself seven sabbatical years–seven years seven times; and they shall be for you, days of the seven sabbatical years, nine and forty years.

Leviticus 25:8

And you shall sanctify the fiftieth year, and proclaim freedom throughout the land for all its inhabitants. A Jubilee it shall be for you, and every man should return to his property, and every man to his family shall return.

Leviticus 25:10

This chapter of the Bible spotlights the agricultural sabbatical year and the jubilee year. Every seven years the Israelites must refrain from working the land and all debts are cancelled by divine decree. The jubilee cycle is the year after seven agricultural sabbatical years—the fiftieth year. All agricultural work is forbidden, all land must be returned to its original owner, and all slaves must be set free. These laws apply only in the land of Israel. What is the point of these laws? What do they mean? What is God trying to teach us—and why do we need both of these different types of special agricultural years?

One commentator looks at the language used to describe the sabbatical year and the jubilee year and compares it to the language used to describe the Sabbath and the holidays. The Sabbath is described as a "resting period"—just like the sabbatical year, and the holidays are described as "holy for you"—just like the jubilee year. The sabbatical year is a cessation of work that is for God, while the jubilee year must be determined, calculated, and declared by the resident High Court of law. Like the holidays, its affirmation and observance depends on us.

What does this distinction mean? He explains that the holidays commemorate the Exodus from Egypt. The jubilee year also commemorates the Exodus from Egypt in a very real way: all slaves must be freed. The Sabbath and the sabbatical year, on the other hand, commemorate the creation of the world.

It is also interesting to notice the recurrence of these patterns throughout the year and throughout the Bible. The same seven-times-seven calculation and celebration is supposed to be observed every year when counting the forty-nine days leading up to the Festival of Weeks. Maybe the jubilee year and the Festival of Weeks have something in common. If the Festival of Weeks commemorates the revelation at Sinai, then perhaps there is something about the jubilee, too, that mimics that. Perhaps God is trying to tell us that there is an inherent connection between the revelation at Sinai and the jubilee commandment to free all slaves and return all land to its original owner. The jubilee year gives us all a chance to start anew, a fresh chance, an opportunity to reconnect with the Bible and God.

A chance to free ourselves.

Cherries Jubilee Cheesecake

Crust
1 cup (230 g) cookie crumbs

¼ cup (60 g) sugar

⅓ cup (75 g) butter, melted

Filling
1½ lb. (720 g) cream cheese, softened

1 14 oz. (396 g) can sweetened condensed milk

4 eggs

¼ cup (60 mL) cherry liqueur

1 tsp. vanilla

½ cup (120 g) cherries from 1 large can or jar of pitted, dark sweet cherries

1 Tbsp. flour

Topping
1 cup sour cream

½ cup sugar

2 tsp. cornstarch

1 Tbsp. sugar

Remaining syrup and cherries

1 Tbsp. cherry liqueur

½ tsp. vanilla

Preheat oven to 325°F (160°C). Grease a springform pan.

Combine crumbs, ¼ cup sugar, and butter. Press into springform pan.

In a large bowl, beat cream cheese with an electric mixer until fluffy. Add in condensed milk slowly. Then add eggs, cherry liqueur, and vanilla. Drain cherries but reserve liquid. Chop ½ cup cherries, toss them with flour, then stir the cherries into cheese mixture. Pour into springform pan and bake for 1 hour and 10 minutes or until set. Remove from oven, allow to cool, and place in refrigerator to chill.

Mix sour cream together with ½ cup sugar and spread on top of cheesecake.

In a saucepan, combine cornstarch, sugar, reserved cherry syrup, cherry liqueur, and vanilla. Cook and stir until thickened. Cool and pour on top of cheesecake. Dot cheesecake with remaining cherries, and serve.

Serves 10–12.

NOTE: If you are unable to find sweetened condensed milk, you can cook 3 cups of regular milk with ½ cup sugar and a dash of vanilla extract and salt until the mixture is thick and reduced by half.

ALTERNATIVES: Make a pretend golden anniversary celebration for God and the world. Purchase fiftieth anniversary plates, balloons, and décor. Concoct a cherries jubilee cocktail and toast your freedom, committing to give yourself a fresh chance.

QUESTIONS: Why do we need to count these years? What is the point of these laws? What do they mean? What is God trying to teach us—and why do we need both of these different types of special agricultural years?

Old and Good

And you will eat things old and aged, and the old you will take out before the new.
Leviticus 26:10

Almost this entire chapter of the Bible is made up of blessings and curses. First the blessings are enumerated (13 verses worth), and then the curses (28 verses worth). When reading through the list of blessings, one comes across the above verse. How can the promise of very old produce be considered a blessing?

One commentator explains that this means that the produce will be well-preserved and grow better with age. Additionally, we will need to clear the storehouses of the old grain and produce because there will be so much abundance that we will need to make room for the new crops. This sounds like an embarrassment of riches. How can it be that three-year-old produce will taste better than freshly harvested grain? Why not just tell us that we will have abundant harvests? Isn't that enough?

Commentators explain that just like we currently value and savor aged beef, aged wine, and aged cheese, the above blessing is akin to that. It's not just that the harvest will be abundant, but that the very nature of the produce harvested will change. Produce will improve with age, just like wine, meat, and cheese do. Similarly, just as wine is valued not only for its physical qualities (taste, color, and aroma), but also for its

spiritual qualities—we bless the Sabbath and holidays over a glass of wine—so too should we value the aged produce and grain as a means of becoming closer to God.

Aged Strawberry Liqueur

3 cups (720 g) strawberries, cleaned, and de-stemmed
1½ cups (300 g) sugar
4 cups (1 L) vodka
1 cup (240 mL) water
1 Tbsp. fresh-squeezed lemon juice

Clean and wash strawberries and place in a bowl. Pour vodka into a clean 64-ounce (2-liter or 8-cup) container and add strawberries, sugar, water, and lemon juice. Cover tightly and let stand in a cool, dark place for 2 days, shaking and turning two or three times per day.

Strain out and discard the pulp. Transfer liqueur to clean container, cover tightly, and let stand for 1 week. Filter one final time, with as fine a filter as you can find—try a coffee filter or fine cheesecloth. Pour into a glass bottle and close tightly. Age for at least 1 month before serving.

Makes 32 oz. (1 liter or 4 cups).

NOTE: This can be done with a variety of fresh fruit—raspberries, peaches, apricots, etc.

ALTERNATIVES: Serve anything aged, from apple cobbler or pie made from "aged" apples in your fridge that were going bad, to the best aged wine, whiskey, steak, or cheese.

QUESTIONS: Why does God enumerate so many blessings and curses in this chapter of the Bible? What is a blessing? What is a curse? Why is eating old produce considered a blessing?

Numbers

Love Counts

Count the heads of all of the congregation of the children of Israel, by their families, by their fathers' houses, number their names, every male, by head-count.

Numbers 1:2

The Book of Numbers is called "the book of censuses" by some and indeed this chapter of the Bible is devoted mostly to a long explanation of the counting process. One commentator states that in the Bible the Israelites were actually counted ten times: When they went down to Egypt (Genesis 46), when they left Egypt (Exodus 12:37), after the incident of the Golden Calf (Exodus 30:12), when they formed their camps in the desert (Numbers 1), when the land was divided (Numbers 26), twice in the times of Saul (I Samuel 11:8, 15:4), during the reign of King David (II Samuel 24:9), in the days of Ezra (Ezra 2:64; Nechemiah 7:66), and the tenth time will be at the end of days.

Why does God feel a need to enumerate his people so many times? One commentator suggests that this was done in preparation for the military campaign they were about to embark upon en route to the land of Israel. He thinks that because the people are counted by their names here, this census gave each person a chance to come before Moses and Aaron and be recognized.

Another commentator's take on this counting exercise is a more emotional one. On the basis of the language used in verse 3, *pakad*, which means to remember or to have concern for, he explains that God was simply counting his people, here and in all the other places, as a way of showing his love for them.

The counting method employed involved the donation of half a shekel from every male over the age of twenty. God employed this method as the ultimate equalizer—every man was required to donate only half a shekel, no more, no less. These contributions were used for the purchase of livestock and other equipment for the communal sacrifices, and no half-shekel alone could make those purchases: the entire community was necessary.

Half-Shekel Carrot Coins

3 cups (680 g) carrots (sliced into rounds, then halved)
¼ cup (60 mL) apple juice
¼ cup (60 g) orange marmalade
1 Tbsp. honey or maple syrup
1 Tbsp. brown sugar
1 tsp. grated orange peel
1 Tbsp. butter or margarine
¼ tsp. salt
¼ tsp. ground cinnamon
¼ tsp. ground nutmeg
1 Tbsp. fresh parsley, chopped (optional)

In a small saucepan, combine carrots, apple juice, and marmalade. Cover and cook over medium heat for 5 minutes, Stir in the remaining ingredients and heat for 5–10 more minutes, or until tender, stirring often.

Serves 4–6.

ALTERNATIVES: Serve any vegetable or fruit that can be sliced into rounds and then halved to represent a half-shekel (cucumber, zucchini, kiwi), serve round cookies (halved), or serve some type of food that can be counted and play counting games—with nuts, seeds, dried fruit, candy, or breakfast cereal.

QUESTIONS: Why does God feel a need to count his people? Why do any of us count anything? What does the process of counting do for us? For others?

Carrying Our Spiritual Weight

This is the service of the Gershonite families–to serve and to carry. And they shall carry the curtains of the Tabernacle and the tent of meeting, and its covering and the goatskin covering overlaid above it, and the screen–the opening of the tent of meeting.

Numbers 4:24-25

The Bible continues with a description of the duties of the Levites, who are grouped by family. Levi had three sons: Gershon, Kohath, and Merari. While Gershon is Levi's firstborn son, we find that Kohath is listed first and given the privilege of carrying the Holy Ark— while Gershon and Merari carry its accoutrements: the screens and tapestries, pillars, bars, and posts.

One commentator claims that the reason Kohath was honored in this way was because he and his family were the most committed to Bible study. Had Gershon been given the honor we would have just assumed that it was because he was the firstborn. This way we question why Kohath was given the honor, and thus we learn about the special honor that is bestowed upon those who toil in the study of the Bible.

To be a priest you must come from the tribe of Levi. A firstborn son is simply born first. But the Bible is accessible and available to all. This is why the honor of carrying the ark was given to Kohath—to show us that Bible study and the honors that go along with it are accessible and available to everyone.

Another commentator explains that the three sons of Levi correspond to the three spiritual levels that people can attain. The family of Kohath represents people who are on the highest spiritual level: they carry the ark. Gershon is on the middle level: responsible for carrying the curtains that divide the Holy of Holies from the rest

of the sanctuary. This is the common man stuck between the divine and the everyday. Merari carries the heavy beams and pillars of the Sanctuary and represents the lowest spiritual level, where spirituality is heavy and burdensome.

The tribe of Levi teaches us how to attach ourselves to God. First we must understand that by engaging in Bible study we can all attain the level reached by Kohath. But we must also remember that no matter what spiritual level we find ourselves at, we all have a role to play in the "carrying of the ark"—wherever we happen to be on the spiritual food chain.

Lace Cookies

For all of us who find ourselves somewhere in the middle—like the tribe of Gershon.

1 cup (240 g) flour
1 cup (240 g) nuts, finely chopped
½ cup (120 mL) corn syrup
½ cup (113 g) butter or margarine
⅔ cup (150 g) brown sugar
1 cup (240 g) chocolate, melted, for dipping and
    decoration (optional)

Preheat oven to 400°F (200°C).

Blend flour and nuts. Bring corn syrup, butter or margarine, and sugar to a boil in a saucepan over medium heat, stirring constantly. Remove from heat; gradually stir in flour and nuts. Drop batter by level teaspoonfuls about 3 inches or 7 cm apart onto a lightly greased baking sheet.

Bake only 8–9 cookies at a time. Bake about 5–6 minutes, remove from oven and allow to stand 5 minutes to harden slightly before removing from baking sheet.

Makes 2–3 dozen cookies.

ALTERNATIVES: Dress your table with lacy fabrics, decorate with curtains, decide to make Bible study a part of your meal once a week, and carry some heavy wooden objects around, just to get a feel for all the different levels of spirituality.

QUESTIONS: Why was each tribe assigned a different task? Why was anyone required to carry anything at all? What do you think the various parts of the Tabernacle represented? Do people in your family all have different tasks and chores? Why?

Dishes of Desire

We remember the fish that we ate in Egypt for free,
the cucumbers, the melons, the leeks, the onions, and the garlic.

Numbers 11:5

It is said that the book of Genesis is a book of transformation: "And God divided between the light and the darkness" (Genesis 1:4). However, there are commentators who say that this also refers to the Book of Numbers, which separates between those who left Egypt and those who came to the land of Israel. This is a transformation that takes place over the course of the entire book and explains why, in this chapter, the Israelites reminisce about Egypt and all its free culinary delights in the form of fish, cucumbers, melon, leeks, onions, and garlic.

Yet there are commentators who question the use of the word "free" in verse 5. If straw was not given to the Israelites in Egypt for making bricks, why would they be given fish free of charge? So the commentators say that what the Israelites missed was being free of the obligations of the laws that God gave them. The food they ate in Egypt didn't have any strings attached.

It is also asked why they specifically missed these foods. The manna was supposed to taste like anything they wanted—so why couldn't it take on these flavors? Though one commentator's answer is a bit strange—he claims that manna couldn't taste like these foods because their flavors are harmful to nursing mothers—his question is right on the mark. It seems like there may be a different layer of explanation underneath this superficial complaint. Perhaps, as commentators explain, the Israelites were not on the spiritual level

they needed to be in order to appreciate the manna.
Manna was a sublimely perfect food; so perfect that
it removed all desire from the eating process. The
people complained because they wanted to *want* food—
especially pungent and sensual food like garlic, onions,
and watermelon—even if it meant that desire was one
of those foods' side effects.

Cucumber and Melon Gazpacho

2 large cucumbers, peeled and seeded
1 melon, peeled and seeded
¼ cup (60 g) fresh dill, chopped
¼ cup (60 g) fresh mint, chopped
2 Tbsp. white wine vinegar
2 cloves garlic, peeled
2 scallions, diced
1 cup (240 mL) carrot juice (if not available,
    substitute orange juice)
1 cup (240 g) plain yogurt
2 Tbsp. olive oil
Salt and pepper, to taste

Finely dice half of 1 cucumber and 1 slice of melon and set aside. Chop the remaining cucumber and melon roughly and put into a blender with the dill, mint, vinegar, garlic, scallions and half the carrot juice. When smooth, mix in the remaining juice, yogurt, and oil. Season to taste with salt and pepper. Refrigerate. Serve garnished with a bit more yogurt and olive oil (as pictured), or diced cucumber and melon, and a sprig of dill.

Serves 4–6.

ALTERNATIVES: You can really plan your entire meal around these simple yet delicious ingredients: fish, cucumbers, melon, leek, onion, and garlic. Here's one simple suggestion: cucumber salad, leek soup, fish with onions and garlic, and melon for dessert. You could also have your guests guess which items of food at your table were mentioned in the Bible, or, alternatively, make a dish that reminds you of home.

QUESTIONS: What do the Israelites mean here by the word "free"? Were these foods they ate truly "free"? What are the foods that are native to the place where you live? What foods would you miss if you were to leave your country? What do you think all these foods have in common?

Great Grapes

And they came to the valley of Eshkol and they cut from there a branch with one cluster of grapes, and two carried it on a pole, and from the pomegranates and from the figs.

Numbers 13:23

In this chapter of the Bible we are told that "in the days of the ripening of the grapes" (Numbers 13:20), the Israelites sent spies down to the land of Israel to scout it out.

Why is it important that we know this detail? Did God specifically choose this time of year to have the spies go down to Israel because he knew there were ripe grapes? One commentator explains that in Hosea (9:10) the Israelites are compared to grapes, and that the ripening of the grapes symbolizes the fact that the time for the redemption had arrived—they had ripened as a people.

Yet the spies go down to the land, return with monstrous fruits and wild tales, and speak slanderously about the land, rather than praising her bounty. According to another commentator, we bring the first fruits on the Festival of Weeks to atone for the sin of the spies. Because they spoke negatively about the land, we must express our love of the land.

The first fruits, he explains, are only brought from the fruits of the seven species—the fruits that the land of Israel is praised for. But the spies brought back pomegranates, figs, and a bunch of grapes, only three of the seven species.

The challenge of the spies was to search out the good in the land and praise that, and they failed miserably in their task. We may no longer "atone" for their sin by bringing the first fruits to the Holy Temple, but we can be careful with the language we use when speaking about the land of Israel, and in our own way, try to find the good in the land.

Spy Fruit Salad

¼ cup (60 mL) fresh lime or lemon juice
2 Tbsp. honey
3 Tbsp. minced fresh mint
Zest of 1 lime or lemon, grated
1 cup (240 g) red grapes
1 cup (240 g) green grapes
8 fresh figs, green or purple
1 cup (240 g) pomegranate seeds or 2 Tbsp. pomegranate
    juice if fresh pomegranate is not available
1 honeydew melon, peeled and cut into chunks

In a large bowl, combine the lime or lemon juice, honey, mint, and zest, and mix well. Add the grapes, figs, and pomegranate seeds. Allow the fruit to marinate for 30 minutes.

In another large serving bowl place the honeydew. Pour fruit mixture over honeydew and mix.

Serves 4–6.

ALTERNATIVES: Put out a bowl of grapes, dried figs, and pomegranates (or pomegranate juice if you can't find fresh pomegranates) to represent the fruit the spies returned with from the land of Israel. Or put out fruit that is native to your land. Make sure to praise the fruit!

QUESTIONS: Why do you think the spies chose these fruits specifically? Why did they choose gigantic fruits rather than bring back more normal sized examples? What could their motive have been? Is it ever good to speak badly of something or someone? Does it matter if we speak negatively about inanimate objects? What power do words have?

Holy Plenty

And the earth opened its mouth and swallowed them and their houses,
and all of the men who were with Korach and all their wealth.

Numbers 16:32

The expression "a land of milk and honey" is found
multiple times in the Bible. It is used only in reference
to the land of Israel, except in one place. Datan and
Aviram, Reuben's sons and Korach's co-conspirators,
apply the term to Egypt, in verse 13 of Numbers chapter
16. Commentators explain that those that flourished
in Egypt saw it as a land of plenty. Korach was blessed
with great wealth, as the Babylonian Talmud explains,
"Joseph hid three treasures in Egypt. One was revealed
to Korach, one was revealed to Antoninus son of Asviros,
and one is hidden away for the righteous in the end of
days." It also states elsewhere that it took three hundred
mules just to carry the keys to Korach's treasure stores.

But what Korach and company all failed to realize is
that Israel's plenty, its "milk and honey" (Deuteronomy
11:9) is not only material. It is said of the land of Israel
that "the fruit of the land are fat with milk and sweet
as honey." The land of Israel is said to be "higher
than all other lands" because of God's blessing. One
commentator even writes that the manna that fell from
heaven in the desert to sustain the Israelites never
really ceased to fall. The manna followed them into the
land of Israel and until today its special nature infuses
the food of the land of Israel with holiness.

Korach corrupted the assembly with food and drink—excessive eating and drinking—so the very land that he, Korach, and his co-conspirators were so quick to disparage opened up and swallowed them whole.

Crater Cake

8 oz. (240 g) bittersweet chocolate
⅓ cup (75 g) butter or margarine
4 Tbsp. orange or berry liqueur (optional)
4 eggs, separated
¾ cup (180 g) powdered sugar
1 tsp. vanilla
¼ tsp. salt
1½ cups (360 g) whipping cream or
    nondairy whipping cream (optional, as garnish)

Preheat oven to 325°F (160° C). Spray non-stick spray on springform pan.

Cut chocolate into pieces. Place chocolate and butter or margarine in a small saucepan on a low flame. Melt, stirring frequently. Add liqueur if using.

In a large mixing bowl, beat egg whites with an electric mixer until foamy. Continue beating and slowly add ½ cup sugar, 1 tablespoon at a time. Beat just until soft peaks form when beaters are lifted, but whites are not stiff.

In another bowl, whisk egg yolks with remaining ¼ cup sugar just until blended. Slowly whisk in lukewarm chocolate mixture, vanilla, and salt. To lighten batter, using a spatula, stir 1 cup of whites into chocolate mixture. Then, gently fold in remaining egg whites just until streaks of egg white disappear. Pour batter into pan and smooth top.

Bake in center of oven until cake is puffed and cracked, and center no longer wobbles when pan is given a gentle shake—about 30–40 minutes. Run sharp edge of a knife around edge of pan to loosen cake. Leave sides on pan and refrigerate, uncovered, until chilled, at least 2 hours. Remove sides from pan, and serve with whipped cream (optional).

Serves 8–10.

ALTERNATIVES: Make a small incision down the center of any loaf or round cake to represent the opening in the earth, earthquake parfaits can be made by layering pudding and cookie crumbs—anywhere you take a bite the earth caves in!

QUESTIONS: What horrible thing would someone have to do to make the earth swallow them whole? What responsibilities does a leader have? When is power used for a good thing? For a bad thing? Can one lead and still stay humble? Is there such a thing as wanting too much power? Can such desires cause earthquakes? Did Korach and his men deserve what they got?

A Cloud of Protection

And Moses did as God commanded him, and they went up Mount Hor before the eyes of the entire congregation. Moses then removed Aaron's garments and dressed Eliezer his son in them, and Aaron was gathered up, and he died there.

Numbers 20:27-28

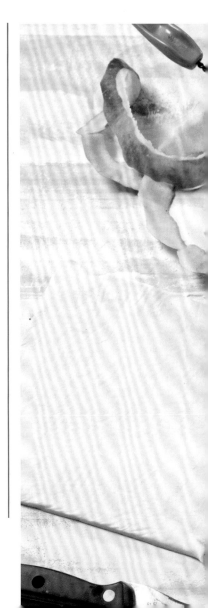

The mountain that Aaron, Moses, and Eliezer climb in this chapter is called *Hor Hahar* in Hebrew. It is a strange expression, and not the way a mountain is usually described. Mount Sinai is called Har Sinai, so Mount Hor should be referred to as Har Hor. The expression Hor Hahar would be better translated "Hor the Mountain." Commentators attempt to explain this strange terminology. According to them, Hor Hahar was named such because it looked like there was one mountain on top of another mountain, a small apple on top of a big apple.

Aaron allows himself to be stripped of his clothing and have it passed on to his son, who will take over for him as the High Priest. Yet this is also strange. Why must we be told that Aaron got undressed—and stayed undressed? According to commentators, Moses told Aaron to take off his clothes and hand them to his son. Then he told him to enter the cave, where a ready-made bed and a lit candle were waiting for him. Moses then told him to get onto the bed, stretch out his hands, close his mouth, and shut his eyes. Moses and Eliezer then left the cave, and the cave entombed Aaron.

After Aaron dies, all of Israel weeps for him for thirty days. The Babylonian Talmud states: "Three great leaders arose in Israel. They are: Moses, Aaron, and Miriam. Because of them, three gifts were bestowed upon Israel: The well, the pillar of cloud, and the manna. The well was provided in the merit of Miriam, the pillar of cloud in the merit of Aaron and the manna in the merit of Moses." After Aaron dies, the Israelites not only lost a great leader, but they would never again be protected by a pillar of cloud.

Apple Mounds in Pastry Dough

1 cup (240 g) ground nuts
½ cup (120 g) sugar
1 tsp. cinnamon
1 pkg. (approx. 17–19 oz./½ kg) puff pastry dough
4 apples, peeled, halved, and seeded
¼ cup (60 g) apricot or marmalade jam
1 egg, beaten
Whipping cream (optional)

Preheat oven to 350°F (180°C).

Mix nuts, sugar, and cinnamon together. Cut puff pastry dough into 6-inch (15 cm.) squares. Spread dough with jam and sprinkle with nut mixture. Place two apple halves in the center of the square—round part down—one on top of the other. Gather up the dough, and twist and pinch edges together. Flip over and place on greased baking sheet lined with foil (so that the pinched seam is on the bottom). Reshape if needed so that it resembles a "mountain." Brush with beaten egg and sprinkle with ground nut mixture. Bake for 30 minutes or until golden brown and puffy. Serve warm with whipped cream "clouds" as decoration (optional). Present them whole for the effect, but cut them in half to actually serve each person.

Serves 6–8.

ALTERNATIVES: Serve rice or mashed potatoes in the form of two mounds or on two separate plates. For dessert you can simply serve one apple half balanced on top of another apple half. Whipped cream can represent the pillar of cloud, or you can have your guests or your kids try to make marshmallow stacks as the pillar of cloud.

QUESTIONS: Why was Aaron told to undress? Do you think he knew that he was going to die? What would you do if you knew when you, or someone you loved was going to die? What would you make sure to do with them or for them? Would you like to be buried on a mountain? Why or why not? Where would you like to be buried? Why?

The Voice of Wisdom

And God opened the mouth of the donkey, and it said to Balaam, "What have I done to you that you have struck me on these three occasions?"

Numbers 22:28

There are only two animals who speak in the Bible: the snake in the Garden of Eden (Genesis 3:1) and Balaam's donkey in this chapter. Fact or fiction, there must be a connection between these two incidents. It seems from the simple meaning of the text in both places that these animals were given the power of speech—which is quintessentially a human characteristic—in order to show the humans in both stories their own lack of intelligence and awareness of the situation at hand.

Adam and Eve led a blessed life in Eden, lacking nothing and living in harmony with their surroundings. The snake however, draws Adam and Eve's attention to the Tree of Knowledge of Good and Evil. It seems that before the snake came along, Adam and Eve hadn't paid the tree very much attention. It is the snake that alerts them to its presence and its power to alter their existence. He shows them that they have a choice to make.

Similarly, for all of Balaam's prophetic abilities, it is his donkey, not he, who sees an angel is blocking their path. Balaam has to whack his donkey three times and the donkey must speak to Balaam to tell him and show him what he cannot perceive. Here too, the donkey is illuminating the choice that stands before Balaam—he may choose to bypass the angel and go forward with his plan, or he may stop now and avoid trouble.

According to one commentator the donkey actually saw the angel while Balaam did not; according to another, it only sensed its presence. Either way, the donkey was able to perceive what Balaam could not. Perhaps in Genesis, too, the snake appears to show us that if we listen to its voice, there is not much that separates us from the animals. Perhaps God caused the donkey to speak to teach Balaam "that the mouth and the tongue are in God's power," a potent lesson for Adam and Eve, and for all of mankind.

Three-Bean Burritos

Burro means donkey in Spanish, and the three beans represent the three blessings that Balaam gave the Israelites.

½ cup (120 g) onion, chopped

2 cloves garlic, crushed

1 Tbsp. oil

½ cup (120 g) canned kidney beans, drained (reserve ½ cup liquid)

½ cup (120 g) canned black beans, drained

½ cup (120 g) baked beans in tomato sauce

Salt and pepper, to taste

1 pkg. flour tortillas (about 8–10)

1 cup (240 g) shredded cheese

¾ cup (180 g) tomato, chopped

1 ripe avocado, cubed (or you can purchase or make guacamole)

Salsa

Sour cream

Preheat oven to 350°F (180°C).

Cook onion and garlic in oil until tender. Remove from heat and stir in beans, salt, and pepper. Mash bean mixture, adding as much reserved liquid as necessary to achieve desired consistency. To assemble each burrito, spoon ½ cup of the filling onto each tortilla. Top with cheese and chopped tomato. Fold edge nearest filling up and over just until filling is covered. Fold in 2 adjacent sides just until they meet; roll up.

Arrange burritos, seam side down in a baking pan, and top with cheese. Bake, covered, for 10 minutes. Uncover and bake for 5 minutes more. Serve burritos with chopped avocado (or guacamole), salsa, and sour cream.

Serves 4–6.

ALTERNATIVES: Serve three-bean salad, three different dishes of food at your table, serve food that comes from all different types of animals, or serve animal crackers, gummy worms, and animal shaped chicken cutlets. Use these animals as props at your table, give them a voice too.

QUESTIONS: Would you like it if animals could talk? What do you think they would say? What animal would you most like to hear talk? Why? What statement do you think the Bible might be making here about how we should treat animals?

Inherited Wisdom

The daughters of Zelophehad the son of Hepher, the son of Gilead, the son of Machir, the son of Manasseh, of the families of Manasseh the son of Joseph, came forward, and his daughters' names were Mahla, Noah, Hogla, Milca, and Tirza.

Numbers 27:1

When Moses began the process of apportioning plots of the land of Israel to the twelve tribes in this chapter of Numbers, five women, the daughters of Zelophehad, approach him and demand that a portion of land be granted to them since their father died in the wilderness and left no sons. Moses consults with God and is told that women may inherit property if there are no male descendents to make the claim.

What is most unusual about this passage, besides the boldness of these women in standing up to Moses and making such a request, is that we do not know who this man Zelophehad is. In Numbers 15:32, the Bible recounts the episode of the man who deliberately desecrated the Sabbath while the Israelites were traveling in the wilderness by gathering firewood. The Babylonian Talmud explains that this man was Zelophehad, and that he was stoned to death as a punishment for his deed.

It seems strange that his daughters would then make a public spectacle of themselves by demanding to inherit the land of their father, who clearly sinned and was punished in a very public way. However, a bit further on, the Talmud relates the story of a pious man who decided to repair his broken fence on the Sabbath. When he remembered it was the Sabbath, he did not fix it. The Talmud then relates that a *tzelaf* (a single caper bush) grew in the space where the fence was broken and that the man and his family were able to earn a living from its fruit.

One commentator explains that this pious man was a reincarnation of Zelophehad and that through his deed he was able to correct and atone for Zelophehad's sin. It is well known that the daughters of Zelophehad were wise women, they were virtuous and they were well versed in the Bible.

It seems that above and beyond the fact that Zelophehad's sin may have been atoned for spiritually, his virtuous daughters were able to put their father's sin behind them and become learned and respected enough to make a claim in front of all the Israelites, before Moses himself, for property that was rightfully theirs.

Pasta with Capers, Olives, and Pine Nuts

¼ cup (60 mL) olive oil
3 cloves garlic, minced
⅓ cup (80 g) pine nuts
2 cups (480 g) pitted black olives, sliced
3 Tbsp. capers, rinsed
1 Tbsp. fresh basil
1 Tbsp. fresh minced parsley
1 tsp. dried oregano
1 lb. (454 g) bag or box pasta, any shape
Salt and freshly ground black pepper, to taste
Parmesan cheese, grated (optional)

Heat olive oil in a frying pan, add garlic and pine nuts, and reduce heat to low. Cook until pine nuts turn golden brown. Add olives, capers, and herbs, and toss well.

Cook the pasta in salted water until al dente. Drain pasta, then toss with the sauce until well combined. Season to taste with salt and pepper and serve sprinkled with Parmesan cheese.

Serves 4–6.

ALTERNATIVES: Capers are a bit of an acquired taste, but they go well on salad and with chicken and fish. Experiment a bit with this new flavor as a tribute to these remarkable women.

QUESTIONS: Why do you think it was so important that the lineage of the daughters of Zelophehad is mentioned here? Do you think your lineage is important too? Why or why not? Why do you think the Bible mentions the names of all these women too? What might this say about the power of standing up for what you believe in? And about the importance of one's inheritance?

A Golden Opportunity

And we shall bring God's offering, every man who has found a gold article–an anklet, a bracelet, a ring, an earring, or a body ornament–to atone for our souls before God.

Numbers 31:50

After their attack on the Midianite people, the soldiers ask to give a donation to the Tabernacle—the gold jewelry that they took from the Midianite women as spoils of war. This seems a very strange gift. We know that out of the twelve thousand soldiers that went to war, not even one of them was harmed. You would think that the soldiers would want to offer a prayer of thanks, or a sacrifice to God. Why jewelry?

One suggestion is that the soldiers offered up this gift as a means of atonement, not for any sins that they transgressed, but for the improper thoughts that they had when they were amongst the Midianite women. However, unlike with the sin of Ba'al Pe'or (in Numbers 25), where twenty-four thousand soldiers were killed because of their sins with the Midianite and Moabite women, here not even one soldier sinned.

One commentator sees the generous donation, which the Bible tells us amounted to 16,750 shekels of gold, not as an offering of atonement, but rather as a redemption of lives. Because no soldiers fell, they felt an obligation to "redeem" their lives in gold.

Golden Cornbread

1 cup (240 g) flour
1 cup (240 g) yellow cornmeal
½ cup (120 g) sugar
1 tsp. salt
4 tsp. baking powder
1 egg
1 cup (240 mL) milk (or milk substitute—soy milk or
    nondairy creamer)
¼ cup (60 mL) oil

Preheat oven to 400°F (200°C). Grease a 9-inch (23 cm) round or 8 x 8–inch (20 cm x 20 cm) baking pan.

Combine flour, cornmeal, sugar, salt, and baking powder. Stir in egg, milk, and oil until well combined. Pour batter into prepared pan and bake for 20–25 minutes, or until a toothpick inserted into the center of the loaf comes out clean.

Serves 6–8.

ALTERNATIVES: Decorate your table with gold—a gold tablecloth, gold napkins, gold paper goods and cutlery. You can also serve other golden foods: golden grahams, golden syrup, golden raisins, golden delicious apples, Rold Gold pretzels, Yukon Gold potatoes, honey, gold wrapped chocolates, Goldschlager, etc.

QUESTIONS: Why do you think gold was chosen as the gift of choice? Why do you think that the Israelites thought that giving a piece of jewelry would atone for their souls? Would you have given something? Why and why not? What would you have given? What do you think is the proper way to atone for something?

Journey On

And these are the journeys of the children of Israel who left the land of Egypt in their legions, by the hand of Moses and Aaron. And Moses recorded the stages of their journeys according to the word of God, and these were their journeys, each stage.

Numbers 33:1-2

The Bible recounts the forty-two places that the Israelites encamped during their exodus from Egypt to the land of Israel. They journeyed from Raamses all the way to the plains of Moab with a whole bunch of stops in between, including the Red Sea, the Zin Desert, Elim with its twelve fountains of water and seventy palm trees, the Sinai Desert, Kadesh (where Miriam died), Hor Hahar (where Aaron died) and more. Some of the stops are described in detail; others are just mentioned by name. Some make sense geographically; many make no sense at all. Why is this long recounting necessary at all?

One commentator uses a parable to explain the significance of this biblical itinerary. The retelling could be compared to a story of a king whose child was ill. The king took his child to a place where he could be healed, and on the return journey, the father recounted to his son all the stops they made on the way: "Here we slept," "Here we caught cold," "Here your head hurt." Similarly here, God is recounting the Israelites's journey through the desert.

Another commentator says that we should look at it as forty-two stages of growth that the Israelites needed to go through as a nation before they could reach the land of Israel. Still more commentators explain that these encampments were not ends unto themselves, but way stations and stepping stones through which

the people progressed on their way to attaining the Promised Land. Every stop is called a journey, even though it was just a place to sleep. Similarly, in life we have pauses, interruptions, and setbacks—many of which we remember fondly, and others which we don't; but each experience we have shapes us as people and aids us in attaining our ultimate goals.

Trail Mix

2 cups (480 g) cereal (Cheerios, Quaker Oat Squares, Chex, or similar)
2 cups (480 g) pretzels
1 cup (240 g) raisins (or assorted dried fruit)
1 cup (240 g) peanuts (or cashews or other nuts, or sunflower seeds, etc.)
1 cup (240 g) M&Ms (or other candy-coated chocolate)
1 cup (240 g) banana chips

Mix together well and store in a large jar or ziplock bag. Portion out into small bags for the road.

Serves 4–6.

ALTERNATIVES: Energy bars, granola bars, ready-made trail mix, any other type of food items meant for traveling like dried fruit and nuts. You can also create a trail with raisins, chocolates, nuts, or fruit and recount every step of your journey as you eat.

QUESTIONS: The Bible recounts the forty-two places that the Israelites encamped during their exodus from Egypt to the land of Israel. Some of the stops are described in detail; others are just mentioned by name. Some make sense geographically; many make no sense at all. Why is this long recounting necessary at all? Is there value in remembering and recounting a journey that you took? What can it help you do?

Deuteronomy

Count Your Lucky Stars

*The Lord, your God, has multiplied you, and here you are
today as numerous as the stars in the heavens.*
Deuteronomy 1:10

When Moses compares the Israelites to the stars in the
sky in this chapter of Deuteronomy, he does so after
reminding the people that he once told them that he
"cannot carry them alone." One commentator asks a bit
of a funny question; rather than take Moses's statement
as a metaphor meaning "you people are as numerous
as the stars in the sky," he takes the verse literally
and asks why Moses compared the Israelites to the
stars in the sky when it is clear that they are not as
numerous. At the time, the people only numbered about
600,000. He provides an answer, explaining that Moses
compared them to the stars as a way of explaining to
them that they would exist forever, like the stars.

A more pointed question might have been, if Moses
already told the people that he couldn't lead them
alone, why did he need to emphasize how much they
had grown and reiterate what he already said? Another
question might be why does he choose to compare the
people to the stars in the sky, when in other places he
compares them to grains of sand? One commentator
points to the strange use of the Hebrew word *eicha* in
verse 12 as a way of answering these questions.

He explains that the word *eicha* is used in three
places: by Moses in this verse in Deuteronomy, in the
first chapter of Isaiah (verse 24), and by Jeremiah
in the first verse of the Book of Lamentations. These
three prophets bore witness to the experiences of the

Israelites at three different milestones: in their glory, when they were like stars; in their sinfulness, as seen by Isaiah; and during their downfall, when the Holy Temple was destroyed. The Hebrew word *eicha* expresses wonder and amazement. Moses asks, "How can I alone bear the burden of your troubles and strife?" in amazement that while he cannot carry the people through it all, God can and does.

Constellation Cookies

Cookie Batter

¼ cup (57 g) butter or margarine

¼ cup (50 g) sugar

1 tsp. vanilla extract

1 tsp. almond extract

Pinch of salt

1 egg

1⅓ cups (320 g) flour

1½ tsp. baking powder

Filling

1¼ cups (300 g) ground nuts (walnuts, pecans, or almonds)

⅓ cup (80 g) sugar

Pinch of salt

1 Tbsp. melted butter or margarine

2 Tbsp. water

1 Tbsp. maple syrup

Preheat oven to 400°F (200°C).

Make the batter by creaming butter and sugar; blend in vanilla, almond extract, salt, and egg. Add flour and baking powder and mix well.

To prepare the filling, combine ground nuts, sugar, and salt. Add melted butter, water, and maple syrup. Mix well.

Roll out dough to approximately ½ inch (1 cm) thickness. Cut with star-shaped cookie cutter. Place a teaspoon of filling in the center of each star and bring the 5 points upright. Pinch sides together so points stand up and allow filling to show. Bake for 7–10 minutes or until light golden brown.

Makes 2–3 dozen cookies.

ALTERNATIVES: Star fruit, fruit cut with a star cookie cutter, salami, tofu, or veggies can all be cut in star shapes; star shaped pasta.

QUESTIONS: Why are the Israelites numbered like the stars when it is obvious that they are not as many as the stars? Why would someone want to be compared to a star? In other places the Israelites are compared to grains of sand. What do you think is the difference? What would you rather be compared to? Why?

Gotta Have Faith

And it will be, when the Lord, your God will bring you to the land he promised to your fathers, to Abraham, to Isaac and to Jacob, to give to you: large and good cities that you did not build, and houses full of all good things that you did not fill, and cisterns that you did not hew, vineyards and olive trees that you did not plant, you will eat and you will be satisfied.

Deuteronomy 6:10-11

Immediately after these verses, Moses gives the Israelites a warning: "Take heed that you do not forget God who freed you from the land of Egypt, the house of bondage." The people just spent forty years in the desert, relying only on God for their sustenance. They witnessed countless miracles as they were taken out of Egypt and given the Bible. What is Moses so worried about?

One commentator says that this warning is given because the people are only human. When one is given everything on a silver platter, it is human nature to become complacent, to lust after one's passions and to forget God. When there is no need to build or grow, when everything comes without effort, it is easy to become full of pride.

Yet the Israelites did not forget God in the desert, though manna fell from the sky and God provided everything they needed. So why would they forget God in the land of Israel—when their "free" crops would rely on God for rain? What is even more interesting is to compare our verses here with some verses later in Deuteronomy. There, Moses again warns the people that they will come into the land, "a land of wheat, and barley, and vines and fig trees, and pomegranates, a land of olive oil and honey, a land where you shall eat bread without scarcity, where you shall not lack anything" (8:8–9), and warns them yet again to "take heed that you do not forget the Lord your God" (8:11). The difference here, however, is that the Israelites have worked for what they have, they have "built fine houses to live in" and their "herds and flocks have multiplied" (8:12–13).

It seems to make more sense that one might forget God here, when one has worked the land and built one's home, and it might be easy to attribute success to one's own efforts rather than God's benevolence.

In fact, it is a matter of perspective. Moses is trying to tell the people that there are many different scenarios that they might encounter in the land of Israel. They may dwell in a portion of land where everything goes well for them, where they must do very little and live off the fat of the land. Others might have to work harder to cultivate their plots of land, to build their homes and tend their flocks. There is danger in both scenarios that one might forget God.

Moses wants the Israelites to understand that faith is hard to maintain no matter what and to impress upon them that faith is the most important thing that they should take with them when they enter the Promised Land.

Tuna with Olive-Wine Sauce

2 garlic cloves, crushed

1 Tbsp. olive oil

1 cup (240 mL) white wine

¼ cup (60 g) black olives, chopped

¼ cup (60 g) green olives, chopped

2 Tbsp. fresh lemon juice

1 tsp. orange zest

Crushed red pepper flakes, to taste

4–6 tuna steaks

Salt and black pepper, to taste

In a large frying pan, sauté garlic in olive oil for 2 minutes. Add wine, olives, 1 tablespoon lemon juice, orange zest, and red pepper flakes. Cook 5 minutes and remove from pan; reserve. Sprinkle tuna with remaining lemon juice, salt, and pepper. Heat pan to high temperature and cook tuna 5 minutes per side. Add sauce and cook 1–2 minutes more per side or until tuna reaches desired degree of doneness.

Serves 4–6.

ALTERNATIVES: Serve grapes, grape jelly/jam, or good wine, olives, olive oil, or an olive spread.

QUESTIONS: What warning is Moses trying to give the Israelites here? What is he afraid of? Why this list of things that were not done? And why will they eat and be satisfied anyway? How important is it to have faith?

Iron Men

It is a land in which you will eat bread without scarcity–where you will not lack for anything; a land whose stones are iron, and from whose mountains you will quarry copper.

Deuteronomy 8:9

Throughout the Bible we are told that the land of Israel is a land of plenty, but usually it is described as a land rich with a certain seven species of grain and fruit, or a land flowing with milk and honey. In this chapter we learn something new—it is also a land rich in iron and copper.

The Babylonian Talmud also picked up on the fact that this comment about the land's stones and mountains seems a bit out of place. It even suggests that we not take this verse literally. It says that instead of reading the word *avaneha* as "the Land's stones," we should read it as *boneha* "the Land's builders." The Talmud explains that "any scholar who is not as tough as iron is not a scholar," and the builders of the land of Israel are its Bible scholars.

However, stone is also extremely strong. Why aren't the Bible scholars compared to stones or to some other strong material? What's so special about iron? The Talmud goes on to explain that Bible scholars are compared to iron because of the way that they learn— they sharpen one another, just as iron sharpens iron. When stone hits stone, fire is created.

Another commentator takes it further, and comments that the reason these Bible scholars are mentioned in conjunction with verses 7–8 which describe the plenty of the land of Israel is because they

are hard as iron in being able to resist the land's plenty. Despite the abundance in the land, the Bible is their sustenance. Perhaps the copper that we quarry is their wealth of knowledge—the strength that our religious leaders may impart to us if we choose to seek it out.

Iron-Rich Black Bean Soup

For the rest of us who are not strong enough to resist the temptations of the Land, black beans are a terrific source of iron.

1 onion, chopped
4 cloves garlic, crushed or minced
1 Tbsp. ground cumin
2 Tbsp. oil
2 15 oz. (425 g) cans black beans, undrained
2½ cups (590 mL) chicken broth
1 large (28 oz./794 g) can stewed tomatoes, undrained

Sauté onion, garlic, and cumin in oil for 3–5 minutes. Add black beans, chicken broth, and tomatoes. Bring to a boil, then reduce heat to low. Simmer 30 minutes.

Let cool and then puree to the consistency you like. Serve, topped with sour cream or grated cheddar cheese (optional).

Serves 6–8.

ALTERNATIVES: Buy or make and serve chopped liver or baked beans.

QUESTIONS: What is the value of iron or copper? Do you consider someone who has lots of iron or copper a rich man? Can a land's mineral resources be as valuable as its produce? What is special about iron?

Soul Food

When the Lord, your God, expands your boundaries, as was promised to you, and you say, "I will eat meat," because your soul desires to eat meat, you may eat meat, according to the desire of your soul.
Deuteronomy 12:20

The above passage is the only place in the entire Bible that speaks about any kind of all-pervasive desire for a specific food—namely meat. The commentators grapple with trying to understand precisely what is meant by this statement. Why are the Israelites now allowed to eat meat? Were they not allowed to eat meat before? What is the change that occurred, and why is it the "soul" that desires meat, and not the body?

One commentator explains that the Bible is teaching us how to conduct ourselves properly in this verse. One should not eat meat unless one has a powerful desire for the meat, or unless one lives in abundance and wealth. So it seems that meat should not be a part of our regular diet. But why should this food be so limited? One commentator suggests that if one was to eat meat regularly one might become poor.

Another commentator opines that Moses is explaining to the Israelites that now that they have entered the land of Israel, they must follow the laws of ritual slaughter. When they travelled in the desert, meat that had been killed in other ways was permitted to them. Still another commentator is of the opinion that this verse comes to explain that in the desert, the Israelites were only allowed to eat meat that had been sacrificed, but now that they are entering the land of Israel, they will be able to eat all types of meat—sacrificed or otherwise.

Hasidic thought actually prescribes the eating of meat as the loftiest act of food consumption, because in eating an animal you are elevating not only the animal, but the vegetation that sustained the animal and the ground on which the vegetation grew. Perhaps the reason that our "souls" desired meat when we entered the land of Israel was because it was only when we were settled in the land that we could reach this lofty spiritual level—the level on which we would be able to elevate all of creation through the consumption of meat.

Meat-Lovers Meatballs

Meatballs

1 lb. (½ kg) ground beef
½ cup (120 g) breadcrumbs
1 egg
Salt, pepper, paprika, and garlic powder, to taste
2 lb. (1 kg) pkg. hot dogs, cut into 1-inch (2.5 cm) rounds

Sauce

1 onion, minced
1 clove garlic, crushed
1 Tbsp. olive oil
½ red bell pepper, chopped
1 12 oz. (340 g) jar pineapple jam
1 cup (240 mL) tomato juice
1 Tbsp. red wine vinegar
2 Tbsp. soy sauce
1 Tbsp. dry white wine
1 tsp. ground ginger

Preheat oven to 350°F (180°C).

To prepare meatballs: Mix together ground beef, breadcrumbs, egg, salt, pepper, paprika, and garlic powder. Take each hot dog round and cover it in ground beef so it is encased in the meatball. Place the meatballs in a greased baking dish and bake for 10 minutes, turning once halfway through the baking process.

To prepare sauce: Sauté onion and garlic in oil for 5 minutes. Add red pepper and cook for 3 minutes more. Then add pineapple jam, tomato juice, red wine vinegar, soy sauce, white wine, and ginger. Bring to a boil.

When meatballs are finished baking, place in the sauce and simmer for 10 more minutes.

Serves 6–8.

ALTERNATIVES: BBQ! Have a great big cookout and serve all kinds of meat! Meat, meat, and more meat! You can wrap up 2–3 types of cold cuts into parcels for an appetizer or party snack. You can serve meat for every course of your meal (except dessert . . . unless you serve mincemeat pie!).

QUESTIONS: Have you ever desired something so much that you felt your "soul" cried out for it? What are your favorite foods? Do you like eating meat? Why/why not? Does meat hold a special place in your heart?

Judgment Call

The first of your grain, your wine, and your oil, and the first fleece of your sheep, you shall give
him. For the Lord, your God, has chosen him of all your tribes, to stand and serve in the name of
the Lord, him and his sons, for all days.

Deuteronomy 18:4-5

The tribe of Levi, consisting of the High Priests and
their attendants, did not get a portion of land in Israel.
Instead, in return for the services that they rendered
the Israelites—acting as Priests in the Temple,
overseeing the cities of refuge, teaching the Bible, and,
as we discover in these chapters, acting as judges (17:9),
they received an annual income from the people as
compensation.

This income included certain portions of a sacrificed
animal, grain, wine, oil, and sheep's wool. Meat makes
sense, as does wool, which can be used to make blankets
and garments, but why specifically grain, wine, and
oil? Why not fruits and vegetables? It is actually a trio
of items that is mentioned time and time again in the
Bible as the mainstay of existence.

To receive gifts for services rendered is
understandable when it comes to giving a portion of a
sacrificed animal. The High Priest serves in the Temple,
cleans it, assists with sacrifices—it makes sense. But
it does not make sense to our ears in modern times
that one should give "gifts" to one's judges. It would
be one thing if the gifts were of a set amount, but
commentators explicitly state that the amount of the
grain given to the tribe of Levi ranges from a sixtieth
to a fortieth of the total produce depending on one's
generosity. And certainly when it comes to good wine
or good olive oil, even today one could make a gift of

an extremely good bottle of aged wine as opposed to a mediocre bottle of wine. How is it that the system did not get abused?

When the original court system was discussed in consultation with Moses's father-in-law Yitro, it was stated that the judges must be "capable, God-fearing men—men of truth, who hate injustice" (Exodus 18:21). And here, the judges are instructed specifically, "Do not bend justice and do not give special consideration to anyone. Do not take bribes, since bribery makes the wise blind and perverts the words of the righteous. Pursue perfect honesty, so that you will live and occupy the land that God your Lord is giving you" (Deuteronomy 16:19–20). Apparently, the Levites were not given a portion of land as a constant reminder to them that they serve God and the people, and it is only through that service, and through a just fulfillment of that service, that they merit living in the land of Israel.

Sweet White Wine and Olive Oil Bread

2½ Tbsp. dry yeast
½ cup (120 mL) warm water
1½ cups (355 mL) olive oil
½ cup (120 mL) white wine
¾ cup (180 g) sugar
1 Tbsp. dried rosemary or thyme (optional)
8–9 cups (1920–2160 g) flour
2 tsp. salt
½ cup (120 g) chopped walnuts (optional)

In a large bowl, dissolve the yeast in the warm water. Add olive oil, wine, sugar, and rosemary or thyme. Stir to combine. Sift the flour and salt together, and then add to the yeast mixture. Knead the dough until smooth, and add walnuts. Cover the bowl, and let dough rise until doubled in size, about 1 hour.

Preheat oven to 350°F (180°C).

Cut dough in half and shape into desired shapes. Let rise for another half hour.

Brush loaves with olive oil and bake for about 30 minutes, or until golden brown.

Serves 6–8.

ALTERNATIVES: Serve a good, thick hearty grain bread, good quality olive oil for dipping and sweet white wine. If you have a sheep fleece, it could make an interesting and conversation-sparking tablecloth.

QUESTIONS: What do you think is special about grain, wine, and oil? What role do they play in your life? What do you think your life would be like if you had no home and had to rely only on your neighbors and friends to support you? Do you think you would find it easy to be just?

Flight of Fancy

If you chance upon a bird's nest on your way, in any tree, or on the ground, with young birds or eggs, and the mother is sitting on the young birds or the eggs, do not take the mother with the young. You shall send away the mother, and take the young for yourself, so that it will be good for you, and you will lengthen your days.

Deuteronomy 22:6-7

The Babylonian Talmud makes a very strange statement about the above verses that we find in this chapter of the Bible. These verses describe the commandment to send away the mother bird before taking the eggs from her nest. We are told that someone who says that God's mercy extends to a bird's nest should be silenced, because that statement reduces this commandment to a humane law, rather than a divine decree.

Nonetheless, other commentators all give humane reasons for this commandment. One writes that taking the birds in the presence of the mother would cause great pain to the animal and that there is no difference between the visceral love of an animal for its children and the visceral love of a human being for its children.

He states that the reason for this commandment is so that we shall not be cruel and devoid of compassion, and because it might cause the destruction of a species. Another commentator says that one performs an act of kindness by sending away the mother bird, because one is thereby allowing all birds to continue to reproduce and benefit all of creation. Still others claim that despite the fact that the Talmud tells us not to have compassion, what God is really trying to do is refine our character traits. It does not matter that God has compassion—what matters is that we should have compassion.

The goal of this commandment is sensitivity training. If there is such a large reward for showing kindness to a mother bird, the reward must be much greater for performing even greater acts of kindness to our fellow man.

Crispy Potato Nests Three Ways

Preheat oven to 350°F (180°C). Grease a muffin tin.

Grate potatoes and squeeze out excess liquid. Mix grated potatoes with egg, flour, salt and pepper. Spoon about ¼ cup (60 g) of mixture into greased muffin cups, make an indentation in the center and push potato mixture up the sides a bit. Brush with olive oil. Bake for 20 minutes or until potato nests are golden brown. Remove from oven and top with fillings. (Ground beef works nicely as a topping, as do sour cream and chives, or spinach and feta cheese.)

Mushroom Filling: Sauté 1 chopped onion and 2 cloves of crushed garlic in 1 Tbsp. olive oil. Add 2 cups (480 g) chopped mushrooms, ¼ cup (60 mL) white wine, ¼ cup (60 mL) cream (can be nondairy), 2 tsp. flour, and 1 Tbsp. chopped fresh parsley. Cook 5 minutes or until thickened, add salt and pepper to taste, and spoon on top of potato nests.

Chicken and Sun-Dried Tomatoes: Sauté 1 chopped onion and 2 cloves crushed garlic in 1 Tbsp. olive oil. Add ½ cup (120 g) chopped sun-dried tomatoes in oil, 1 Tbsp. chopped fresh basil, and 2 diced skinless, boneless chicken breasts. Cook until onions are soft and meat is no longer pink. Add salt and pepper to taste, and spoon on top of potato nests.

Roasted Vegetables: Place 1 onion (halved), 1 red pepper (whole), 1 zucchini, 2 tomatoes (halved) and 1 sweet potato (sliced into rings) on a baking sheet. Roast the vegetables at 400°F (200°C) for 15–20 minutes or until nicely browned. Remove peel from red pepper, then chop all the vegetables and mix together with 1 container of tomato paste, 1 Tbsp. olive oil, 1 tsp. dried oregano and/or rosemary, and salt and pepper to taste. Spoon on top of potato nests.

Serves 8–10.

Potato Nests

3 large baking potatoes
1 egg
1 Tbsp. flour
Salt and pepper, to taste
Olive oil

ALTERNATIVES: Create bird's nests with peanut butter and chocolate coated cereal, Chinese noodles, or pretzels, and then use peanut M&Ms for the eggs. Coconut, powdered sugar, and butter melted together can also be used to make nests and chocolate chips make tasty eggs!

QUESTIONS: Do you think it's kind to shoo a mother bird away before taking her eggs? Why and why not? How does this commandment teach us compassion? In what ways are we like birds?

Land of Plenty

And he brought us to this place, and he gave us this land, a land flowing with milk and honey.

Deuteronomy 26:9

Though this verse is by no means the first or the only place in the Bible that we see the land of Israel referred to as a "land of milk and honey," it is the only place where it is mentioned three times (verses 26:9, 26:15, and 27:3). The first time that "milk and honey" is mentioned in connection with the land of Israel is when Moses meets God face to face at the burning bush, where he is told that he will bring the Israelites out of Egypt and into a land of milk and honey (Exodus 3:8, 3:17). Another two references appear in Exodus: in reference to the Passover holiday (13:5), and after the sin of the golden calf (33:3). The term is also found in Leviticus (20:24), and in Numbers. When the spies speak badly about the land of Israel, they mention that it is indeed a land flowing with milk and honey (Numbers 13:27, 14:8), and a reference is also made during Korach's rebellion (16:13, 16:14), and then in Deuteronomy (6:3), and again in 11:9 and 31:20. This brings us to a grand total of fifteen times that the land of Israel is called a land of milk and honey.

Why is it that the land of Israel is repeatedly referred to as the land of milk and honey? Why not cattle and sheep, fruits, grain, and wine—all of which are mentioned in connection with the land of Israel as well?

The first time that milk and honey are mentioned in connection with the land of Israel, in Exodus (3:8), one commentator suggests that God uses this terminology as a way of explaining that the land itself is of good quality. There are green grassy meadows and good fresh air, because animals only produce lots of milk when they live in favorable conditions, and these favorable conditions also produce luscious fruit that drips with honey. Another commentator contends that God is trying to explain through these two food items that the Israelites will live in wealth and prosperity in the land, because milk and honey are delicacies, luxury products that can only be afforded by the well-to-do. This same commentator states in Deuteronomy (26:9) that when the Israelites left Egypt, God told them that the land was flowing with milk and honey so that they would understand that he was not just taking them to any land, but to the choicest of lands.

Still another commentator raises an interesting point in his commentary on Deuteronomy 26:15. God promises the land of Israel to Abraham, Isaac, and Jacob in Genesis, yet the fact that this is a land of milk and honey is not mentioned even once in the entire book of Genesis. It is only to Moses and to the generation of people that are taken out of Egypt that God not only promises the land, but, a land that will flow with milk and honey for all eternity.

Milk and Honey Kugel

1 16 oz. (454 g) pkg.
   medium egg noodles
⅓ cup (75 g) butter
½ cup (120 mL) honey
2 tsp. salt

2 tsp. vanilla sugar
½ cup (120 mL) cream or
   milk
5 eggs

Preheat oven to 350°F (180°C).

   Boil and drain noodles, and return to pot. Add butter, honey, salt, and vanilla sugar. Mix well. Add cream or milk and eggs. Mix well. Pour mixture into a baking dish and bake for 1 hour or until kugel is golden brown and firm to the touch.

Serves 8–10.

ALTERNATIVES: Serve hot steamed milk to drink and flavor it with honey. Put honey on top of ice cream, or yogurt, or make honey ice cream! Add honey to your cereal or even add it to your coffee with the milk!

QUESTIONS: Why is it that the land of Israel is repeatedly referred to as the land of milk and honey? Why not cattle and sheep, fruits, grain, and wine—all of which are mentioned in connection with the land of Israel as well?

Heartthrob

Lest there be among you a man, a woman, a family, or a tribe, whose heart has strayed today from God, to go and worship the deities of other nations.

Deuteronomy 29:17

In these chapters of Deuteronomy we find the word "heart" mentioned ten times. As Moses has been doing for most of the book of Deuteronomy, he continues with his narrative in which he gives over his parting words to the Israelites. He calls for the people to enter into a new covenant with God and warns against their hearts straying from faithfulness to God by serving idols. What is interesting is that God refers to the heart as being what strays.

Furthermore, the feelings of the heart are central throughout this entire section of the Bible. God promises that if we take the blessings and curses to heart and return to God with all our hearts, he will bring us into the land of Israel, where he will circumcise our hearts. Moses also impresses upon the people the accessibility of the Bible, saying that it is near to us, in our mouths, and in our hearts. Why is this relationship, this covenant that the Israelites are about to enter into with God, a duty of the heart? And why is the heart the lynchpin of our relationship with God?

One commentator states that at the core of following God's precepts is the heart; it is the essential element. Another commentator explains further that when it comes to distinguishing between truth and falsehood, you can only do so with your heart. You can intellectualize all you want, but knowing the difference between good and evil is something instinctive.

Still another commentator explains that desire stems from the heart, and that God helps us to return

to him only if we desire it with our whole heart. God promises that if we return to him with our whole hearts, someday he will circumcise our hearts, which, he explains, means that God will remove the desire that causes us to sin.

But another commentator explains that many of God's commandments have a verbal element to them so that the mouth helps the heart to remember, and a physical element—an action—to help remind the mouth what it is supposed to say. Therefore, Bible study and keeping God's commandments are "duties of the heart," because doing the right things, helping our friends and connecting to God, is really on the "tip of our tongues" and already instilled in our hearts.

Hearts of Palm Soup

1 onion, chopped
2 cloves garlic, minced
1 leek, diced
2 Tbsp. olive oil
2 15 oz. (450 g) cans hearts of palm, drained and diced
2 cups (475 mL) water
½ cup (120 mL) white wine
1 Tbsp. chicken or vegetable soup powder
Salt and pepper, to taste
1 cup (240 mL) cream

Sauté onion, garlic, and leek in olive oil for 5 minutes or until soft. Add the hearts of palm and sauté 2 more minutes. Add water, wine, and soup powder. Simmer 15 minutes. Add salt and pepper, and remove from the heat. Stir in the cream slowly in a steady stream, and continue stirring until combined. Puree soup with an immersion blender or in a food processor until smooth. Return to pan and reheat on a low flame.

Serves 6–8.

ALTERNATIVES: Hearts of palm and artichoke hearts go great in salads, and you can use Romaine hearts to make the salad. Cucumbers can be cut into heart shapes and always season everything with a little love.

QUESTIONS: What do you feel with your heart? What things do you feel without your heart? How do you act upon the feelings of your heart? In what ways do you make your feelings real? Do you let your heart guide you?

Scroll Responsibilities

And Moses wrote this scroll, and gave it to the priests, the sons of Levi, who carry the Ark of the Covenant of God, and to all the elders of Israel.

Deuteronomy 31:9

There are many different opinions about how the Bible was written. One suggestion is that Moses wrote the Bible one section at a time. In these last chapters of the Bible we are witness to Moses's completion of the Bible. Most commentators also cite this chapter as the source for the final commandment in the Bible—the commandment to "write" a Bible "scroll."

When Moses finishes speaking to the Israelites, God tells him to "write for yourselves this song and teach it to the people; put it in their mouths, in order that this song may be my witness against the children of Israel" (Deuteronomy 31:19). One commentator suggests that the "song" refers to the poem that begins in chapter 32. Another commentator explains this verse to mean that every person must write a scroll that contains the song in chapter 32 that begins, "Give ear, O heavens, and I will speak; and may the earth hear the words of my mouth."

Some say that even if you inherit a Bible from your father, you must still write one of your own. But according to some commentators, even writing your own Bible is not enough. The point is that we make sure that we "put it in their mouths" (31:19), meaning that we must teach the Bible to our children so that it "will not be forgotten from the mouth of their offspring" (Deuteronomy 31:21). We must make sure that we teach the Bible and its lessons to our children so that they know it well enough to teach others.

Jelly Roll Bible Scroll Cake

4 large eggs, separated, at room temperature
1 cup (240 g) sugar
1 Tbsp. vanilla extract
1 cup (240 g) flour, sifted
1 tsp. baking powder
¼ tsp. salt
½ cup (120 g) powdered sugar
1 cup (240 g) jam
1 8 oz. (237 mL) container whipping cream

Preheat oven to 400°F (200°C).

Line a jelly roll pan or cookie sheet (with a rim) with parchment paper. Beat egg yolks with an electric mixer until light. Add in the sugar and vanilla and mix well. Add flour, baking powder, and salt, and mix until just combined. In a separate bowl, beat egg whites until stiff peaks form. Fold 1 cup of egg whites into egg yolk mixture and then fold in the rest of the egg whites. Pour onto parchment paper and smooth out. Bake for 8–10 minutes or until cake is golden and springs back when touched.

When cake comes out of oven, dust the top of the cake with powdered sugar and place another sheet of parchment paper on top. Invert pan so that cake is on top of the new sheet of parchment paper. Trim off edges so that the cake is uniform in size. Roll cake up into a spiral and let cool.

Beat cream until stiff. Unroll cake gently and spread with jam and whipping cream, then reroll without top parchment paper, removing bottom parchment paper as you roll.

Serves 10–12.

ALTERNATIVES: Wafer roll cookies, elephant ear cookies, and pinwheel cookies all have a "scroll" look and feel to them. It is also possible to buy a jelly roll cake instead.

QUESTIONS: Why do you think we need to write our own Bible scrolls? What do you think the Bible means when it says we each need to write our own song? What do you think it means to "put it in our mouths"?

Rained Out

My discourse shall come down like the rain, my speech will drop like dew, like a shower on leaves of grass, like droplets on leafy herbs.

Deuteronomy 32:2

For the most part, and especially in the land of Israel, rain is seen as a tremendous blessing. Moses compares rain to the Bible, according to one commentator, because both provide life to the world. Rain gives joy to the whole world, including birds and animals, he says. Yet this commentator admits that while rain makes most people rejoice, not everyone welcomes the rain. He explains that travelers, wine-filled cistern owners, and others might not rejoice in the coming of the rain. Therefore, he says that the second clause of Moses's sentence is important because dew pleases everyone.

A different commentator sees the rain as representing the written Bible and the dew as the oral law. One comes down from heaven (rain) and the other is visible and present only on the earth (dew). Similarly, the Bible was dictated to us by God through Moses, but the oral law is Moses's explanations on how to put God's dictates into practice.

Commentators also view the two expressions as two different ways that people absorb information. Some need the information driven into them; they need to be drenched by it, as though by a hard rainfall. Others absorb in a more gentle manner, and need to be taught and spoken to in a more discreet, less direct way. Both rain and dew are critical for the proper growth of certain plants. Similarly, we hope that

the Bible in all of its forms will bring about spiritual growth in all those that adhere to its precepts, no matter how hard they like their rain to fall.

Honeydew and Rainforest Fruit Salad

1 honeydew melon, diced

1 mango, diced

1 cup (240 g) pineapple, diced (fresh or canned)

3 kiwis, peeled and diced

1 cup (240 g) macadamia or cashew nuts

1 cup (240 g) dried bananas

¾ cup (180 g) flaked coconut

2 tsp. lime juice

1 Tbsp. orange juice

1 Tbsp. honey

1 Tbsp. coconut milk

½ tsp. vanilla

Mix together honeydew melon, mango, pineapple, and kiwi in a large bowl. Top with macadamia or cashew nuts, dried bananas, and flaked coconut. Mix together lime juice, orange juice, honey, coconut milk, and vanilla. Before serving, pour dressing on top and serve immediately.

Serves 6–8.

ALTERNATIVES: You could serve "rain"-drop soup, rainy day stew, or a good cup of hot cocoa if it is actually raining outside!

QUESTIONS: What kind of rain is a blessing? What kind of rain is a curse? Is rain always welcome? When do we want it to rain? When do we want it to stop? What is your favorite kind of rain? What is your favorite way to learn? Do you think that the two are connected?

A Return to Eden

And Israel shall dwell securely alone, Jacob's blessing, in a
land of grain and wine; and the heavens will drip dew.
Deuteronomy 33:28

We have reached the end of our culinary journey
through the Bible. The above verse comes after Moses
delivers his blessings to all of the twelve tribes. But it is
a bit of a strange blessing. Why is it a blessing to "dwell
securely alone"? And why the afterthought of "also, the
heavens will drip dew," which changes the tense of the
sentence.

One commentator explains that every individual
will live under his own vine and fig tree, and that the
people will be so secure that they will not live clustered
together in groups as in cities or towns, but they will
feel so safe that they will spread themselves out all over
the land. He explains that the use of the word "and"
comes to explain that Isaac's blessing of "dew of the
heavens" was added to Jacob's blessing.

These last chapters also represent the culmination
of one major event in the Bible: Adam's banishment
from the Garden of Eden. When the Israelites settle the
land of Israel—the land "of grain and wine"—they are
being reinstated into a Garden of Eden of sorts. Yet one
commentator explains that the blessing was to be of the
people on the land, rather than the land on the people.
This means that the people are the ones to impart the
blessing onto the land and, through their actions, have
it well within their power to restore Israel to its original
Eden status.

Red Wine and Barley Salad

2 cups (475 mL) water
1 cup (240 g) barley
½ small red onion, diced
1 small red pepper, chopped
1 cup (240 g) cherry tomatoes, quartered
1 cup (240 g) red grapes, pitted and halved
1 Tbsp. chopped fresh parsley
1 tsp. dried oregano
½ cup (120 g) slivered almonds, toasted
¾ cup (180 g) crumbled feta cheese

Dressing
1 Tbsp. Dijon mustard
4 Tbsp. red wine vinegar
⅓ cup (80 mL) olive oil
Salt and pepper, to taste

Bring the water to a boil and pour the dry barley in. Cook until all the water has been absorbed or until barley is soft—about 30–40 minutes. Let the barley cool and then toss with all the salad ingredients except the cheese.

Mix together dressing ingredients. Pour dressing over salad and fold cheese in carefully. Serve immediately.

Serves 6–8.

ALTERNATIVES: Serve hearty grain bread and good wine to toast your having finished your culinary journey through the Bible! Serve foods that signify the Garden of Eden to you—whether they be your favorite recipes or something that symbolizes a return to a purer, more spiritual state.

QUESTIONS: Do you think it's safe to dwell alone? Would you want to live alone? With your family? In a big city of town? Where do you think is the safest place to live? Do you think that people determine if a city is safe or not?

Biblical Ingredients

Please note, while I did attempt to be as thorough as possible, this is not a comprehensive list. It was compiled mainly to shed light on the recipes in this cookbook, highlighting foods that appear most frequently in my recipes, with some interesting extras for demonstrative and anecdotal purposes.

Almonds (Genesis 43:11)—*"take from the best of the land in your vessels and bring the man a gift: a little balsam, a little honey, some gum and resin, pistachios and almonds."* Almonds are mentioned numerous times in the Bible, but often it is the "almond blossom" rather than the nut itself that is referred to. For example, the Menorah is described as being made up of "cups" that have the shape of almond blossoms, and Aaron's rod is said to have blossomed with ripe almonds. Almonds are mentioned most directly as a food item in the Genesis verse quoted above, where Jacob sends gifts down to Egypt to his son Joseph, the viceroy of Egypt.

Barley (Deuteronomy 8:8)—*"a land of wheat and barley, and grapes and figs and pomegranates; a land of olive oil and honey."* Barley is one of the five grains mentioned in the Bible that is native to the land of Israel. It is also one of the seven species that characterize the land of Israel. Barley is also one of the specific grains mentioned that was affected by the plague of locusts that was sent by Moses and God to afflict the land of Egypt.

Bread (Genesis 18:5)—*"And I will fetch a loaf of bread, and you will feast until your heart is content."* Even though bread's origins are of an unfortunate nature: when God exiles Adam and Eve from the Garden of Eden with the curse "by the sweat of your brow you will eat bread" (Genesis 3:19), it is not for naught that bread is considered to be the mainstay of our meals and that most meals are begun with some form of "breaking bread" ritual. It is unclear how much bread in biblical times resembled the many varieties and types of breads we eat today, but it is clear that bread is as central to our meals and lives today as it was in biblical times. When there was famine in Egypt, Joseph was able to provide bread for his family. When Abraham welcomed guests to his tent, bread was the first thing he offered them, and of course, Jacob served Esau bread with his lentil stew.

Butter (Genesis 18:8)—*"And he took curd, and milk, and the calf which he had dressed, and set it before them; and he stood by them under the tree, and they did eat."* The modern Hebrew word *"hemah"* is the word for butter. The word *"hemah"* in the above verse is usually translated as "curd" but sometimes as butter. It is clear that the Israelites must have formed some type of curd, cheese, or spread from the milk that they had in abundance, perhaps similar to the "labaneh" or "leben" cheese of today, but it was likely a product of goat's milk or sheep's milk, rather than the cow milk butter we are most familiar with today.

Cinnamon (Exodus 30:23)—*"and take for yourself choice spices, myrrh five hundred shekels, and sweet cinnamon half as much, two hundred and fifty, and of calamus two hundred and fifty."* Cinnamon is considered one of the finest spices in the Bible, alongside myrrh and cassia and is used as a major component of the anointing oil that was used to sanctify both the priests and the Tabernacle furnishings. Evidence of the potency of cinnamon is that only half as much was needed to impart fragrance to the perfumed oil. Indeed, even just a small amount of cinnamon imparts a very unique and discernible taste and scent to any recipe.

Coriander (Exodus 16:31)—*"And the house of Israel named it manna, and it was like a white coriander seed, and its taste was like a wafer of honey."* Coriander is mentioned twice in the Old Testament and both times in connection with the description and consistency of the manna. Coriander is an interesting spice in that its leaves are used as an herb in many recipes (often called cilantro in this form and popular in Mexican cuisine), but its seeds have a completely different flavor, consistency, and use and can be used ground or whole.

Cucumbers (Numbers 11:5)—*"We remember the fish that we ate in Egypt for free, the cucumbers, the melons, the leeks, the onions, and the garlic."* Cucumbers are mentioned in the Old Testament only once, in the above verse, and only as a food that the Israelites lament that they miss when they leave Egypt. It is unclear if the cucumbers mentioned here bear any resemblance to the cucumbers of today, and the Hebrew word used *"kishuim"* is the modern Hebrew word for zucchini or squash, but in this verse, cucumber is the most common translation of the word.

Dates (Exodus 15:27)—*"And they arrived at Elim where there were twelve springs of water and seventy date-palms; and they camped there, by the waters."* While dates are most commonly enumerated among the seven species of the land of Israel, they are actually only mentioned in the Old Testament by name one time, in the above verse, and here it is the date-palm tree referenced, rather than the fruit itself. Because the date is so sweet, and when dried can often ooze honey, it is often made into silan (date honey). When the seven species are mentioned in the Bible, the date is often referred to as "date honey" or even just as "honey." The consensus nonetheless is that it is date honey that is being referred to, not honey from bees. There are some who say that this applies to the honey mentioned in the phrase "a land of milk and honey," that the honey referenced here is date honey and the milk is goat milk (which is certainly much more indigenous to the land of Israel than cow milk).

Eggs (Deuteronomy 22:6)—*"If you chance upon a bird's nest on your way, in any tree, or on the ground, with young birds or eggs, and the mother is sitting on the young birds or the eggs, do not take the mother with the young."* Oddly enough, this is the only mention of eggs in the Old Testament, and they are not mentioned specifically as a food item, but rather, it seems, more in connection with the taking of the live baby birds from the nest. However, the very fact that eggs are even mentioned here at all seems to imply that there was some use for them in biblical times, though they are never once explicitly mentioned in the Bible as permitted or not permitted for consumption.

Figs (Numbers 13:23)—*"And they came to the valley of Eshkol and they cut from there a branch with one cluster of grapes, and two carried it on a pole, and from the pomegranates and from the figs."* Figs are mentioned in the Old Testament in a few ways. One, as part of the seven species which characterize of the land of Israel, a second time, in connection with the incident of the sending of the spies down into the land. The spies apparently brought back figs so enormous that the Israelites were afraid of the land as a result. The fig leaf is of course most famously associated with Adam and Eve in the Garden of Eden who are most often portrayed as having covered themselves with fig leaves upon becoming aware of their nakedness.

Fish (Genesis 48:16)—*"May the angel who redeems me from all harm bless the youths, and may they be called by my name and the name of my fathers, Abraham and Isaac, and may they multiply like fish, in the midst of the land."* Besides being mentioned in the form of a blessing, fish are discussed in the Old Testament numerous times: they are the first live creatures to be mentioned during the creation story in Genesis, they inhabit the rivers that turn to blood in Egypt during the plagues, they are recalled as a food item that the Israelites lament and miss when they leave Egypt, and fish are listed as part of the permitted and forbidden foods. What is interesting is that no specific species of fish are mentioned in the Old Testament, as is done with birds and other animals. Fish are only mentioned in general, the only specification made is that all fish with fins and scales are permitted to be eaten.

Garlic (Numbers 11:5)—*"We remember the fish that we ate in Egypt for free, the cucumbers, the melons, the leeks, the onions, and the garlic."* Garlic is mentioned in the Old Testament only once, in the above verse, and only as a food that the Israelites lament that they miss when they leave Egypt.

Goat (Genesis 27:9)—*"Go now to the flock, and take for me from there two good kid goats; and I will make from them savory foods for your father, like he loves."* What is interesting about this mention of goats in the Old Testament is that the goat is one of the only animals that is discussed as a food item, rather than a sacrifice. Certainly most of the sacrifices were eaten by someone, even if only the High Priest, but here the goat is mentioned as being made into a meal with no ceremonial or ritual aspect to it other than being tasty. Of course Jacob then uses this meal to steal the birthright from Esau, but in its simplest form, it's just food, and food that Isaac apparently loved. Perhaps we should all give goat meat another chance . . .

Grain (Deuteronomy 18:4)—*"The first of your grain, your wine, and your oil, and the first fleece of your sheep, you shall give him."* While wheat and barley are the two grains enumerated as part of the seven species of the land of Israel, when the Old Testament mentions grain it is often translated as corn, but it is unclear if this is the type of corn that we think of today as it is unlikely that it was native to the region at that time. The five grains native to the land of Israel are often translated as: barley, wheat, rye, spelt, and oats, but these are not all mentioned by name in the Old Testament, and it is unclear if these grains were actually cultivated in the land of Israel in biblical times or if these are just the translations that we give to words that actually represented a different species of grain entirely.

Grapes (Leviticus 19:10)—*"And your vineyard, do not glean, nor gather the fallen grapes of your vineyard; leave them for the poor and for the stranger: I am the Lord your God."* There are so many places that grapes, grapevines, wine, raisins, and grape derivatives are mentioned in the Bible that it is difficult to know where to begin! Grapes are one of the seven species of the land of Israel, they are one of the fruits of enormous size that the spies brought back from the land of Israel in an attempt to blaspheme the land, grapes are mentioned as a crop—as an example of how to glean your fields, as a warning about how to interact with your neighbors, and as a beverage, both alcoholic and not.

Honey (Deuteronomy 26:9)—*"And he brought us to this place, and he gave us this land, a land flowing with milk and honey."* Honey is mentioned as one of the seven species characteristic of the land of Israel. However, the consensus is that it is date honey that is being referred to, not honey from bees. Honey is also mentioned fifteen times in the Bible in the phrase "a land of milk and honey," but there are those who say that the honey referenced here is also date honey. Nonetheless from other sources and references, it does seem likely that wild bee honey was available during the times of the Bible.

Hyssop (Leviticus 14:4)—*"As the priest commands, he shall take for the person that needs to be cleansed: two live, pure birds, a cedar stick, a strip of crimson wool, and hyssop."* Not to be confused with the modern hyssop plant, this herb or plant was more likely a form of the Middle Eastern herb za'atar, which is a form of oregano. Hyssop is used in three important biblical ceremonies: in the ceremony for the purification of a leper, in the red heifer ceremony which imparted purity to all those who are ritually impure from coming in contact with a dead body, and by the

Israelites in marking their doorposts with blood so that God would "pass over" their homes during the plague of the smiting of the firstborn of Egypt.

Lamb (Exodus 12:21)—*"And Moses called for all the elders of Israel, and said to them: 'Draw out and take a lamb for your families and slaughter the Passover offering.'"* While lambs are most commonly referenced in the Old Testament in connection with sacrifices, there are quite a few places where lambs are singled out for mention. The Israelites are commanded to take a lamb and tie it to their bedposts and then slaughter it for the Passover offering. When Abraham sets off to sacrifice Isaac, Isaac innocently asks, "where is the lamb for the offering?" to which Abraham replies, "God will provide the lamb, my son," and the two of them go on their way. Lambs are also mentioned in the Old Testament in connection with shepherding. Both Abraham and Jacob act as shepherds to herds of lambs.

Leek (Numbers 11:5)—*"We remember the fish that we ate in Egypt for free, the cucumbers, the melons, the leeks, the onions, and the garlic."* Leeks are mentioned in the Old Testament only once, in the above verse, and only as a food that the Israelites lament that they miss when they leave Egypt.

Lentils (Genesis 25:34)—*"And Jacob gave Esau bread and a stew of lentils; and he ate and drank and got up and went on his way."* Though it is clear that lentils and other beans and legumes were a mainstay of the biblical diet, lentils are the only legume/bean mentioned in the Old Testament and they are only mentioned once, when Jacob shares his infamous "mess of pottage" with his brother Esau.

Locust (Leviticus 11:22)—*"and even of these you may eat: any kind of locust, and any kind of bald locust, and any kind of cricket, and any kind of grasshopper."* Some might say that all of the bugs mentioned in the above verse deserve their own separate listing in this glossary, but since none of these creatures are common fare in modern western cuisine, I will list all of them under the heading of "locust." With all of the animals, birds, and fish that are listed as forbidden in the Old Testament it is indeed surprising that locust, cricket, and grasshopper are not more of a delicacy nowadays. You can find recipes for these succulent insects online if you choose to experiment. Indeed the Middle East was only just recently plagued by a swarm of locusts, though I am unsure if anyone actually partook of the feast.

Mandrake (Genesis 30:14)—*"And Reuben went in the days of the wheat harvest, and he found dudaim in the field and he brought them to Leah, his mother."* While it is unclear if the dudaim mentioned in the Old Testament are indeed mandrakes, it seems to be the most common interpretation, though it has also been suggested that this plant was ginseng root, lotus, jasmine, violet, barley, blackberry, banana, citron, lily, fig, or poppy flowers. Regardless, the mandrake seems a relatively good guess as it grew in the land of Israel at the time of the Bible and still grows there today. The mandrake root contains scopolamine and hyoscyamine, two chemical compounds that may be used as medicines or poisons. Throughout history and in literature, the mandrake root has been hailed as a magic plant, an aphrodisiac, and a fertility drug,

Meat (Deuteronomy 12:20)—*"When the Lord, your God, expands your boundaries, as was promised to you, and you say, 'I will eat meat,' because your soul desires to eat meat, you may eat meat, according to the desire of your soul."* Meat is mostly mentioned in the Old Testament in the form of specific animals: oxen, sheep, lamb, goats, etc. The words for meat in Hebrew is *"basar"* which means "flesh" and it is the same word used when describing the skin or flesh of man himself. There are two main times in the Old Testament when the Israelites cry out to God for "flesh" or meat. In the desert, God answers their cry by flooding the encampment with quail. The other mention of "flesh" or meat comes as in the quote above, a promise that when the Israelites finally arrive in the land of Israel and get settled, they will be able to eat as much "flesh"(meat) as they would like.

Melon (Numbers 11:5)—*"We remember the fish that we ate in Egypt for free, the cucumbers, the melons, the leeks, the onions, and the garlic."* Melons are mentioned in the Old Testament only once, in the above verse, and only as a food that the Israelites lament that they miss when they leave Egypt.

Milk (Deuteronomy 26:9)—*"And he brought us to this place, and he gave us this land, a land flowing with milk and honey."* The phrase "milk and honey" appears in the Old Testament fifteen times, not always in connection with the land of Israel. It seems pretty clear that the milk that is being referred to is goat milk (which is certainly much more indigenous to the land of Israel than cow milk). Milk is also mentioned in connection with the prohibition "do not cook a kid in its mother's milk" and since a kid is a baby goat this also seems to indicate that it is goat milk which is most commonly referred to in the Bible.

Olives (Deuteronomy 6:11)—*"houses full of all good things that you did not fill, and cisterns that you did not hew, vineyards and olive trees that you did not plant, you will eat and you will be satisfied."* Olives are actually only mentioned in the Old Testament once as themselves and only then in Deuteronomy as part of a curse. Other than that, Olives are mentioned in the Old Testament always in connection with either olive trees, olive oil, or an olive branch. Regardless, it is clear that olives were abundant in the land of Israel and certainly a part of biblical cuisine.

They are one of the seven species native to the land of Israel and olive oil is critical both for the kindling of the Menorah (candelabra) in the Holy Temple and for use in anointing both the priests and the contents of the Tabernacle.

Olive Oil (Exodus 27:20)—*"And you shall command the Israelites, and they shall bring to you pure pressed olive oil for illumination, for the kindling of light, eternally."* Olive oil is highlighted in the Old Testament in three central ways: as one of the seven species of the land of Israel, as a main ingredient in the anointing oil used to sanctify the High Priest and the contents of the Tabernacle, and as the oil used for the kindling of the Menorah in the Holy Temple. It seems that there were other oils in use in biblical times since every other mention of oil in the Old Testament does not specifically mention "olive oil" which seems to imply that olive oil had a special status in biblical times as the most holy and sacred oil.

Onion (Numbers 11:5)—*"We remember the fish that we ate in Egypt for free, the cucumbers, the melons, the leeks, the onions, and the garlic."* Onions are mentioned in the Old Testament only once, in the above verse, and only as a food that the Israelites lament that they miss when they leave Egypt.

Pigeon (Numbers 6:10)—*"And on the eighth day he shall bring two turtledoves or two young pigeons, to the priest, to the opening of the tent of meeting."* Pigeons are only mentioned in the Old Testament in connection with sacrifices, and therefore it is unclear if they were eaten and regularly enjoyed as a meal.

Pistachio Nuts (Genesis 43:11)—*"take from the best of the land in your vessels and bring the man a gift: a little balsam, a little honey, some gum and resin, pistachios and almonds."* Pistachio nuts are mentioned only once in the Old Testament in the verse quoted above, where Jacob sends gifts down to Egypt to his son Joseph, the viceroy of Egypt. Almonds and pistachios are the only nuts mentioned in the Old Testament. The Hebrew word used for pistachio in the Old Testament is *botnim* which is the modern Hebrew word for peanuts, but the consensus seems to be that the Bible is talking about pistachios here as the peanut was not native to the land of Israel at that time.

Pomegranates (Deuteronomy 8:8)—*"a land of wheat and barley, and grapes and figs and pomegranates; a land of olive oil and honey."* The pomegranate is one of the seven species of the land of Israel. Besides that, it is one of the fruits of enormous size that the spies brought back from the land of Israel, and it also has the distinction of being mentioned as a description of what the decorations on the High Priest's clothing should look like: "pomegranates of blue, and of purple, and of scarlet, around his skirts."

Quail (Exodus 16:13)—*"And it came to pass in the evening, the quails went up and covered the camp; and in the morning there was a layer of dew surrounding the camp."* There are two main times in the Old Testament when the Israelites cry out to God for "flesh" or meat. In the desert, God answers their cry by flooding the encampment with quail. However, the second time this happens, God punishes the Israelites for their gluttony by bringing a plague upon the people.

Raisins (Numbers 6:3)—*"he shall abstain from wine and liqueur: he shall not drink wine vinegar or vinegar liqueur, and he shall not drink any grape juice, and fresh or dried grapes he shall not eat."* Raisins (or dried grapes) are mentioned in the Old Testament only once, in connection with the food items that a Nazirite may not eat. (A Nazirite is someone who takes a vow to abstain from all grape products and alcohol, does not cut his hair, and does not come in contact with any dead bodies, even those of family members.)

Salt (Leviticus 2:13)—*"And you shall season every meal-offering with salt, do not discontinue the salt of the covenant of God from your meal offering—on all your sacrifices you shall offer salt."* While salt is clearly a critical component of all sacrifices—both animals and grain—salt is also most famously mentioned in the Old Testament in connection with the story of Lot's wife who turned into a pillar of salt after looking back at the destruction of the city of Sodom. God also makes a "covenant of salt" with Aaron and the tribe of Levi, promising them that they will always be provided for by tithes from all the other tribes. Salt is clearly valued as a preservative, both for foods and for eternal promises.

Sheep (Deuteronomy 14:4)—*"These are the animals that you may eat: the ox, the sheep, and the goat."* Sheep were obviously a valued commodity during the times of the Bible. Not only are they mentioned as animals that one could sacrifice to God, but they are also specifically enumerated as an animal that is permitted for consumption. Still, sheep are mentioned more frequently in the Old Testament as part of people's herds, and in situations where someone would need to be redressed for a stolen sheep. Sheep are also mentioned as part of women's dowries, as a measure of a man's wealth, and as spoils of war. It seems that sheep were more valuable as possessions than they were as meat, most likely because of the milk and wool that they provided.

Unleavened Bread (Exodus 23:15)—*"For seven days you shall eat unleavened bread as I have commanded you, for the festival of the month of springtime, because you left Egypt then, and you shall not see my face empty-handed."* From the many verses in the Old Testament about unleavened bread, both in connection with the Passover holiday and in connection with grain sacrifices (which were always offered unleavened,) we learn that in the times of the Bible it seems that most of the bread that was eaten was leavened in some way. However, it is unlikely that the "unleavened bread" that was eaten in biblical times actually resembled the "matzah" of today. It was likely much more similar to a tortilla or a very flat soft pita bread, rather than a crunchy cracker or wafer.

Wheat (Deuteronomy 8:8)—*"a land of wheat and barley, and grapes and figs and pomegranates; a land of olive oil and honey."* Wheat is one of the seven species of the land of Israel. It is the most commonly mentioned grain in the Old Testament. The wheat harvest is mentioned multiple times in the Old Testament as a very important time, and the first of the wheat harvest is mentioned in connection with the harvest festival known as the "festival of weeks."

Wine (Deuteronomy 33:28)—*"And Israel shall dwell securely alone, Jacob's blessing, in a land of grain and wine; and the heavens will drip dew."* Wine is mentioned in the Old Testament so many times that it is difficult to even count how many references there are. Wine was clearly a mainstay of the biblical diet, but it was also used ceremonially, and as part of some biblical sacrifices. Noah is famously mentioned in the Bible as the first man to get drunk on wine, and Lot's daughters got him drunk on wine in order that they should conceive. The High Priest is also warned not to drink wine when he participates in the Temple service.

Wine Vinegar (Numbers 6:3)—*"he shall abstain from wine and liqueur: he shall not drink wine vinegar or vinegar liqueur, and he shall not drink any grape juice, and fresh or dried grapes he shall not eat."* Vinegar is mentioned in the Old Testament only once, in connection with the food items that a Nazirite may not eat, which seems to mean that it is wine vinegar that the Bible is referring to. (A Nazirite is someone who takes a vow to abstain from all grape products and alcohol, does not cut his hair, and does not come in contact with any dead bodies, even those of family members.)

Glossary

Food Items and Terms

balsam—term used for various pleasantly scented plant products, and the plants which produce them.

brisket—cut of meat from the breast or lower chest of beef or veal, with beef brisket being considered one of the nine beef prime cuts.

bulgur—cereal food made from the groats of several different wheat species, most often from *durum* wheat. Common in the cuisine of Europe, the Middle East, and South Asia.

capers—edible flower buds, often used as a pickling seasoning, of a perennial winter-deciduous plant that bears rounded, fleshy leaves and large white to pinkish-white flowers. The caper bush is also used in the manufacture of medicines and cosmetics.

charoset—sweet, dark-colored, paste, usually made from fruits, nuts, and wine, traditionally eaten at the Passover Seder. Its color and texture are meant to recall mortar which the Israelites used when they were enslaved in Ancient Egypt.

citron—a fragrant citrus fruit, botanically classified as *Citrus medica* and used ceremonially by Jews on the Feast of Booths.

gum—any of a number of naturally occurring resinous materials in vegetative species.

jasmine rice—long-grain variety of rice also known as "Thai fragrant rice" that has a nutty aroma and a subtle *pandan*-like flavor.

kosher salt—a variety of edible salt with a much larger grain size than common table salt, typically containing no additives such as iodine.

kugel—baked pudding or casserole, similar to a pie or a soufflé, most commonly made from egg noodles or potatoes and used by Jewish cooks from Eastern European descent.

mandrake—common name for members of the plant genus *Mandragora*. The plants contain deliriant hallucinogenic tropane alkaloids such as atropine, scopolamine, apoatropine, and hyoscyamine, leading to their use in magic rituals and contemporary pagan traditions.

manna—edible substance that the Israelites ate during their travels in the desert, provided by God according to the Old Testament. Described as being fine and flaky, white like coriander seed with a taste like cakes baked with oil or wafers made with honey.

pavlova—meringue-based dessert named after the Russian ballet dancer Anna Pavlova, having a crisp crust and soft, light inside. The dessert is believed to have been created in honor of the dancer either during or after one of her tours to Australia and New Zealand in the 1920s.

resin—a hydrocarbon secretion of many plants, valued for its chemical properties and associated uses, such as the production of varnishes, adhesives, and food glazing agents as well as being a constituent of incense and perfume.

za'atar—generic name for a family of related Middle Eastern herbs from the genera oregano, basil, thyme, and savory. Also the name for a condiment made from the dried herb, mixed with sesame seeds, dried sumac, and often salt, as well as other spices. Popular in the cuisine of the Middle East as a herb and a spice mixture.

Sources Mentioned

Babylonian Talmud—central text of Rabbinic Judaism including the Mishnah (the first written compendium of Judaism's Oral Law) and the Gemara (an elucidation of the Mishnah) representing the culmination of more than three hundred years of analysis of the Mishnah in the Babylonian Academies.

Book of Ezra—a book of the Bible detailing the return to Zion after the end of the Babylonian captivity and the rebuilding of the temple in Jerusalem.

Book of Hosea—a book of the Bible, of the "Prophets" section, in particular, the first of the twelve minor prophets. Written at the time of Isaiah who was a contemporary of Hosea.

Book of Isaiah—a book of the Bible from the "Prophets" section, describing the visions of Isaiah son of Amos, describing the doom of the sinful kingdom of Judah as well as the restoration of the nation of Israel.

Book of Jeremiah—a book of the Bible from the "Prophets" section, describing the recorded visions of Jeremiah, who lived in Jerusalem in the late seventh and early sixth centuries BC during the time of king Josiah and the fall of the Kingdom of Judah to the Babylonians, who subsequently went into exile in Egypt.

Book of Lamentations—a book of the Bible written in a poetic style mourning the destruction of Jerusalem and the Holy Temple in the sixth century BC.

Book of Nehemiah—a book of the Bible detailing the rebuilding of the walls of Jerusalem after the end of the Babylonian captivity.

Book of Samuel I and II—books of the Bible from the "Prophets" section detailing the coronation and subsequent history of the Israelites' first kings: Saul and then David. Traditionally considered to be authored by the prophet Samuel.

Jastrow Talmudic Dictionary—popular and comprehensive Dictionary of the Targumim, Babylonian Talmud, Jerusalem Talmud, and Midrashic Literature written by Marcus Jastrow.

Jerusalem Talmud—central text of Rabbinic Judaism including the Mishnah (the first written compendium of Judaism's Oral Law) and the Gemara (an elucidation of the Mishnah) representing the culmination of more than three hundred years of analysis of the Mishnah in the Academies of Israel. Written in a western Aramaic dialect.

Song of Songs—a book of the Bible, also known in English as Canticle of Canticles or simply Canticles, traditionally credited as being authored by King Solomon. A poem between a man and a woman moving from courtship to consummation.

Biblical Characters

Aaron—Moses's older brother who became the High Priest of the Israelites.

Abel—one of two sons of Adam and Eve, he was a shepherd, while his brother Cain was a crop farmer. When presenting their sacrificial offerings to God, Cain is jealous of Abel and murders him.

Abiram—a great grandson of Reuben, who rebelled against Moses and was put to death by fire sent by God.

Abraham—the patriarch in the Old Testament (Genesis), founding father of the Israelites, who played a prominent role in the establishment of Judaism, Christianity, and Islam. In Genesis a covenant is established between Abraham and God.

Balaam—a diviner in the Old Testament who hated the Israelites yet praised them when he saw their array of tents.

Benjamin—the second and last son of Rachel, youngest son of Jacob, who is said to have remained with Jacob when his brothers plotted against Joseph.

Bezalel—the chief artisan of the Tabernacle, the Tent of Meeting, and the sacred furniture.

Cain—one of two sons of Adam and Eve, he was a crop farmer, while his brother Abel was a shepherd. When presenting their sacrificial offerings to God, Cain is jealous of Abel and murders him.

Dathan—a great grandson of Reuben, who rebelled against Moses and was put to death by fire sent by God.

David—depicted as a righteous king of Israel, he was an acclaimed musician, warrior, and poet. He established Jerusalem as the capital of the twelve tribes.

Edom—a geographical area south of the Dead Sea, it also means "red" and was given as a name to Esau, because he "sold" his birthright for a bowl of "red" porridge.

Eliezer—the second son of Moses and Tzipporah, also the name of the man who acted as a marriage broker for Isaac.

Ephraim—one of Joseph's sons adopted by Jacob who formed a tribe in the Northern part of Israel.

Esau—along with Jacob, the sons of Abraham and Rebekah. Although Esau was the firstborn, Jacob was favored. Many believe this was because Jacob was more educated and Esau was a hunter and "rough" man.

Gershon—the eldest son of Levi, founder of the Gershonites who were in charge of the outer Tabernacle.

Gilead—the father of Jephthah, as well as the region east of the River Jordan.

Hepher—the father of Zelophehad.

Heth (Chet)—the Hittites or children of Heth are a people mentioned in the Old Testament. They are listed in Book of Genesis as second of the twelve Canaanite nations, descended from Heth. Heth is said to be the son of Canaan, son of Ham, son of Noah.

Hogla—one of the five daughters of Zelophehad.

Hur—a companion and staunch friend of Moses and Aaron, mentioned as the grandfather of Bezalel.

Isaac—the son of Abraham and Sarah, born when Abraham was one hundred years old. He was the father of Jacob and Esau.

Jacob—the third patriarch in the Old Testament whose children became the twelve tribes of Israel. The son of Isaac and Rebekah, grandson of Abraham and Sarah.

Joseph—the eleventh of Jacob's twelve children, Rachel's son, he wears a "coat of many colors" and is sold into slavery by his jealous brothers. He rises to become the Viceroy of Egypt.

Judah—the fourth son of the biblical patriarch Jacob, forming the biblical tribe of Judah, ruled by the line of King David.

Kohath—a son of Levi, founder of the Kohathites who were one of the four divisions of the Levites.

Korach—a great grandson of Levi, who rebelled against Moses and was put to death by fire sent by God.

Leah—the first of two wives of the patriarch Jacob. She gave him six sons who became six of the twelve tribes of Israel, as well as a daughter, Dina.

Levi—the third son of the patriarch Jacob and Leah and the founder of the biblical tribe of Levites, consisting of the priestly caste.

Lot—a much talked about nephew of Abram (Abraham), the faiths look at Lot differently, he travels with Abraham, he flees the destruction of Sodom and Gemorrah, but he is also intoxicated and seduced by his daughters. He is revered by Christians and Muslims as a righteous man. According to Christianity, Jesus is a descendent of Lot, as is King David, whose great-grandmother was Ruth, a descendant of Lot's son Moab.

Machir—the father of Gilead who also conquers a land called Gilead.

Mahlah—one of the five daughters of Zelophehad.

Manasseh—one of Joseph's sons adopted by Jacob who formed a tribe in the Northern part of Israel.

Merari—a son of Levi, founder of the Merarites who were in charge of the care of the "boards" of the Tabernacle.

Milca—one of the five daughters of Zelophehad.

Miriam—sister of Moses and Aaron, she helps save Moses by arranging for him to be raised by the Pharoah's daughter. She later sings a song at the Red Sea.

Moses—a biblical prophet accepted by all three major faiths. When the Pharoah of Egypt ordered the murder of all Israelite boys, he was hidden in a river and found and raised by Pharoah's daughter. He became a "prince" of Egypt and later led the Israelites to freedom, and into Israel.

Noa— one of the five daughters of Zelophehad.

Noah—in the Book of Genesis, Noah is ordered by God to build an ark, on which he places two of each animal in the world to save them from a flood.

Oholiab—from the biblical tribe of Dan, he worked as a deputy architect with Bezalel specializing in carpentry, weaving, and embroidery.

Pharaoh—title for the ruler of ancient Egypt. The Pharoah who ruled when Joseph became Viceroy is unknown, and we are not sure which Pharoah ruled when Moses led the Israelites on their exodus.

Rachel—described in the Old Testament as the favorite wife of Jacob, one of the three biblical matriarchs. She is the mother of Joseph and Benjamin.

Reuben—the oldest son of Jacob and Leah, he is involved in the plot to "sell" Joseph, and later tries to "save" Joseph (who ends up becoming Viceroy of Egypt.)

Samael (angel)—considered as the guardian angel of the biblical Esau. Some consider him good and others evil.

Sarah—the wife of Abraham and the mother of Isaac. The final saga of Abraham is burying Sarah in Hebron in the book of Genesis.

Tamar—daughter of King David and sister of Absalom. She is raped by her half-brother Amnon, whom Absalom kills in revenge.

Tirza—one of the five daughters of Zelophehad.

Uri—the son of Hur and the father of Bezalel.

Yitro—Jethro, Moses's father-in-law, a Kenite shepherd and priest of Midian.

Zelophehad—one of the men who left Egypt as part of the exodus. He had five daughters and no sons, and influenced Moses to allow his inheritance to go to his daughters, usually not done in biblical times.

Hebrew Words

Adom—Hebrew word for the color red.

Agala—Hebrew word for "cart" or "wagon."

Avaneha—Hebrew word for "her stones."

Azaz— Hebrew for strong, mighty, bold, or prevail.

Boneha—Hebrew word for "her builders" or, as "Baneha," her sons.

Cheres—earthenware, as in a vessel or potsherd.

Chet—Hebrew word for "sin."

Chitah—Hebrew word for "wheat."

Dod—Hebrew word for "uncle," but can also mean "lover" or "dear friend."

Dudaim—"And Reuben went out into the field and found some *dudaim*." Most commonly interpreted as mandrakes.

Egla arufa—An obscure biblical ceremony to determine the murderer by breaking the neck of a calf.

Egla—Hebrew word for "calf," as in a baby cow.

Eicha—biblical word for "lamentations," as in The Book of Lamentations, also translated as the expressions "how can it be?," "where are you?," or "Alas!"

El—Hebrew word for God, also has the connotation of strong or hard.

Hagim—Hebrew word for "holidays."

Hamsa—meaning "five," a palm-shaped amulet in the Middle East thought to provide defense against the evil eye.

Katit—Hebrew word for "beaten," as in beaten olives for olive oil.

Ketonet passim—the "coat of many colors" was given to Joseph by his father Jacob. It is said that this exacerbated the jealousy felt towards Joseph by his brothers.

Lama'or—Hebrew word for "used for lighting," such as a special olive oil for burning for light.

Manna—an edible substance supplied by God when the Israelites were in the desert.

Metzora—Hebrew word for "one being diseased," or a leper as mentioned in Leviticus 14–15.

Moadim—biblical word for "the intermediate days of a holiday," for example, if the Feast of Tabernacles is eight days long, then the first and last days are the actual religious holiday, and the five days in between are the "moadim."

Motzi shem ra—Biblical Hebrew for "the deliberate dissemination of damaging untruths."

Na—a Hebrew word that can mean please, now, or raw (uncooked).

Pakad—Biblical Hebrew for "recalled," as in "remembered."

Shemen—Hebrew word for "oil."

Vayinashcheihu—"and he bit him." (Genesis 33:4) when Esau ran to Jacob after not seeing him for a while. There is doubt as to whether the "kiss" was real or insincere.

Vayishakeihu—"and he kissed him." (Genesis 33:4) when Esau ran to Jacob after not seeing him for a while. There is some doubt as to whether the kiss was real or insincere.

Zach—a Biblical Hebrew word for "pure."

Zayit—Hebrew word for "olive."

Places in the Bible

Azazel—mentioned three times in the Old Testament, it means "who God strengthens." Also referred to as a "scapegoat," a demon, or an undefined location in the desert.

Ba'al Pe'or—an idol associated with Mount Pe'or in the Moab region, also could be the description of a local god whose cult worship was associated with the body's various openings.

Babel—biblical word for the city of "Babylon."

Canaan—the biblical name generally associated with the Semitic speaking area of the Middle East.

Eden—biblical name for the Garden in which Adam and Eve were placed.

Elim—biblically near the eastern shore of the Red Sea, it was one of the places the Israelites encamped when they left Egypt.

Eshkol—an area in the northwestern Negev in Israel.

Gilead—the biblical name for the region located east of the Jordan River.

Hebron—a "holy city" located south of Jerusalem, especially noted for Abraham's purchase of the Cave of the Patriarchs.

Hermon—a cluster of mountains in the Golan Heights.

Kadesh—biblically the Wilderness of Kadesh, located in the Aravah section of the Negev, Israel.

Machpelah—the Cave of the Patriarchs in Hebron, Israel, which Abraham purchased to bury the patriarchs.

Mamre—a biblical market city north of Hebron, Israel.

Mount Hor (Hor Hahar)—either a mountain on the eastern shore of the Dead Sea, or a mountain on the northeast shore of Israel on the Mediterranean Sea.

Mount Sinai—the mountain upon which Moses received the Ten Commandments. Its exact location is unknown.

Plains of Moab—biblically the eastern shore of the Dead Sea.

Raamses—an Egyptian city in biblical times at which Israelites were enslaved at hard labor.

Red Sea—located in the Great Rift Valley, its borders include the Suez Canal and the Sinai Desert.

Sinai Desert—the section of Egypt east of the Suez Canal.

Sodom—biblical city near the Dead Sea which was destroyed by God's fire for being synonymous with impertinent sin.

Zin Desert—biblically the Wilderness of Kadesh, located in the Aravah section of the Negev, Israel.

Miscellaneous

Day of Atonement—also known as Yom Kippur, this twenty-five hour fast day is mentioned in the Old Testament and is generally considered the holiest day of the biblical year, a day of atonement for sins and repentence.

Festival of Weeks—one of the three biblical pilgrimage festivals, usually in May/June, signifying the anniversary of the giving of the Ten Commandments and the beginning of the grain harvest.

Golden Calf—as Moses ascended Mount Sinai to receive the Ten Commandments, some Israelites lost faith and created an idol in the form of a calf made of gold. Upon his discovery of the Golden Calf, Moses smashed the Ten Commandments against the calf and went back up to Mount Sinai to plead for a second chance.

High Priests—the chief religious officials of the biblical Israelites, tracing their ancestry back to Aaron, brother of Moses. Their responsibilities "ended" with the destruction of the Holy Temple in Jerusalem by the Romans in 70 AD.

Holy Ark—also known as the Ark of the Covenant—a chest described in the Old Testament which held the stones on which the Ten Commandments were written.

Holy of Holies—the inner Sanctuary of the Tabernacle and later the Holy Temple in Jerusalem.

Holy Temple—also known as the Temple in Jerusalem, this was historically the site of worship for ancient Israelites and later the Jewish people.

Jubilee—a biblically prescribed holiday occurring every fifty years involving ownership and management of land.

Levites—the descendants of the tribe of Levi, with Aaron as their patriarch.

Midianite People—a people who were descendants of Abraham through his wife Keturah.

Moabite People—the people living in a tribe east of the Dead Sea.

oral law—in the Jewish tradition, the written law was the Old Testament as given by God to Moses. All the discussions about this were included in the "oral law."

Passover—one of the three biblical pilgrimage festivals usually celebrated March/April commemorating the departure of the Israelites from Egypt.

Rosh Hashana—a two-day biblical holiday celebrating the anniversary of the creation of Adam and Eve. It is celebrated with festive meals, blowing of the ram's horn (shofar), and pensive worship.

Sabbath—"and God rested on the seventh day." From Genesis, a day prescribed by God for physical rest and spirituality.

Shekel—an ancient form of currency, used especially to form the census.

Tabernacle Festival (or Feast of Tabernacles, Feast of Booths)—one of the three biblical pilgrimage festivals, usually in September/October, signifying the end of the harvest season.

Tabernacle—the biblical portable dwelling place for the Divine as worshipped by the Israelites.

Ten Commandments—also known as the Decalogue, a set of biblical laws encompassing ethics and worship, holy to Judaism, Islam, and Christianity.

Acknowledgments

This cookbook began in Dublin, Ireland. I know, that's a pretty strange place for a cookbook about the Bible to begin, especially since I currently live in Jerusalem, and I spent a large part of my childhood in Israel. But my cookbook began there, at the home of Judy Charry and Carl Nelkin, where I had a simple bowl of red lentil soup on the weekend when the weekly portion we had read and discussed was Genesis 25. I was fascinated by the concept: What if there was a way to bring every chapter of the Bible alive with food? The year was 1998, I was a student at Trinity College Dublin, and on Saturday night on my way home from their house I bought a notebook and started to write down my ideas.

I wrote down ideas for about five years, it was often silly things like "Rainbow Cookies!!" and "dove + olive branch = ?" but sometimes I made really meaningful notes that I would use later to develop my recipes, things like "Death of Aaron – Hor Hahar – like apples? Mound of something? Aaron entombed – so something wrapped in puff pastry?" and "Coriander seed + Honey doughnut?"

It wasn't until 2005, while working at *The Jerusalem Report* for David Horovitz, that I discovered I had a knack for writing about food, and it wasn't until 2006 that as editor of *The Jerusalem Post*, David gave me the chance to finally put all my years of note-taking to good use. The scribbles in my notebook became computer files of ideas, which transformed into a weekly column, entitled "The Weekly Portion," which ran in *The Jerusalem Post* for over two years.

It was my readers who convinced me to turn these columns into a cookbook—the fans who kept writing to the newspaper for six months after I decided to stop writing the column begging me to come back and start writing again.

It was my friends who encouraged me over the years with jokes like "is this cake called Death By Chocolate?" and "how holy is this Angel Food Cake?" and of course everyone who taste-tested my recipes both when I was writing my weekly column and when I was perfecting each recipe for inclusion in this cookbook.

Thank you to Charmaine Gruber for providing a first copyedit of my manuscript.

But it was really Malka Margulies of the Salkind Agency who made me believe that this was actually going to happen on the day that she offered representation, and Neil Salkind, who doggedly continued to pursue the publication of this cookbook, long after I had almost given up hope. Malka and Neil, thank you. This book is as much yours as it is mine.

And after all that, it was editor extraordinaire Joseph Sverchek at Skyhorse who took a chance on me and made me believe that I would actually hold a copy of my cookbook in my hands this year.

I must also thank everyone at The Deborah Harris Agency: Deborah Harris, George Eltman, Ines Austern, Sharon Katz, Efrat Lev, Ilana Kurshan, Michal Banit, and Ran Kaisar who not only put up with my many absences from work during my photo shoots, but were gracious enough to eat and compliment the leftovers after every shoot. Special thanks to Ran who introduced me to my photographer, Boaz Lavi.

Boaz, there are no words. Not only did you do an incredible job, often bringing me to tears because I could not believe that you were able to make my food look so incredible, but you also taught me so much about food photography that I will never look at a cookbook the same way again. The reason this cookbook looks so amazing is only because of you. Thank you for the laughs and the good humor, your ability to work under pressure and to improvise and get the best shot every time, and especially for your incredible talent and artistic eye.

Thank you also to Leiba Rosenberg Costello, my sous-chef for most of the photo shoots. I couldn't have done it without you. Thanks also to Alida and Miles Bunder, my parents, for the use of their spacious home, two kitchens and gardens, as well as general help in the kitchen during the photo shoots, and carving advice and expertise when it came to the meats. Thank you to all my other friends who came to help with the cooking and cleaning during the many photo shoots: Elana, Libi, Shira, Simone, and Chana. And a special thank you to Dina Grossman, without whom the Gingerbread Mishkan would never have happened.

Of course one might say that this cookbook really began in 1981, when my parents, Alida and Miles, who are so central to my life, first took my family to the land of the Bible, and then moved my family to Jerusalem for five formative years that would affect all of our lives in ways we never imagined. My parents are directly responsible for cultivating in me a love for food, from fine wines that always graced our table, to teaching me about spinach and liver, brussels sprouts and cauliflower, at a very young age, and also for taking me with them everywhere, to the finest restaurants on South Beach, for the best hand-churned ice cream on Lincoln Road, and to the best fish-hut on Key Biscayne. Everything I am and everything I have accomplished is because of you, who always believed in me and always taught me that I could do anything I wanted if I tried hard enough. I learned to cook at my mother's elbow, who in turn learned to cook at her mother's elbow. Ema, everything I know about the kitchen I learned from you. And to my father who always said to me "writers write, always" and was right, of course, as usual.

To Jonathan who has supported me in every endeavor, from crazy trips across Europe to feasts in Montreal where no weekend went by without our serving fifty of our nearest and dearest friends. Through five very difficult pregnancies which resulted in our five unique and incredibly special children, and for being the most hands-on father I know, which has enabled me to stay sane, keep writing, and always pursue my dreams, often at the expense of your own. Thank you. I love you forever.

And last but not least to my kids, who I have no doubt will someday look back on all these crazy years and realize how rich all these projects of mine have made our lives, but at the time might not have seen it that way. I know I'm doing something right though, because all of you love both food and books in your own ways. If nothing else, I've done that right. Nachliel, Avtalyon, Lehava, Shaanan, and Nehorai: I love you always.

Index